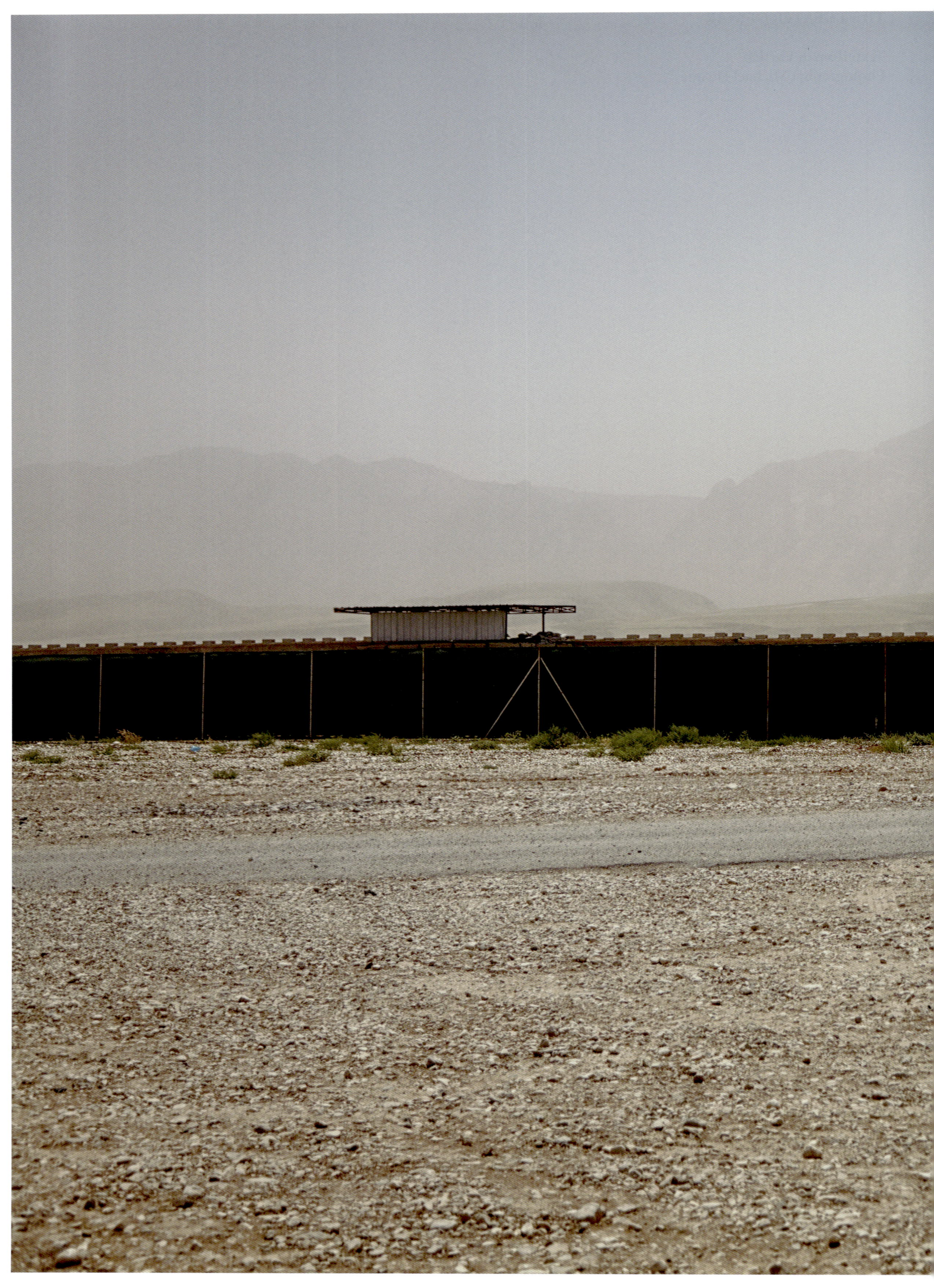

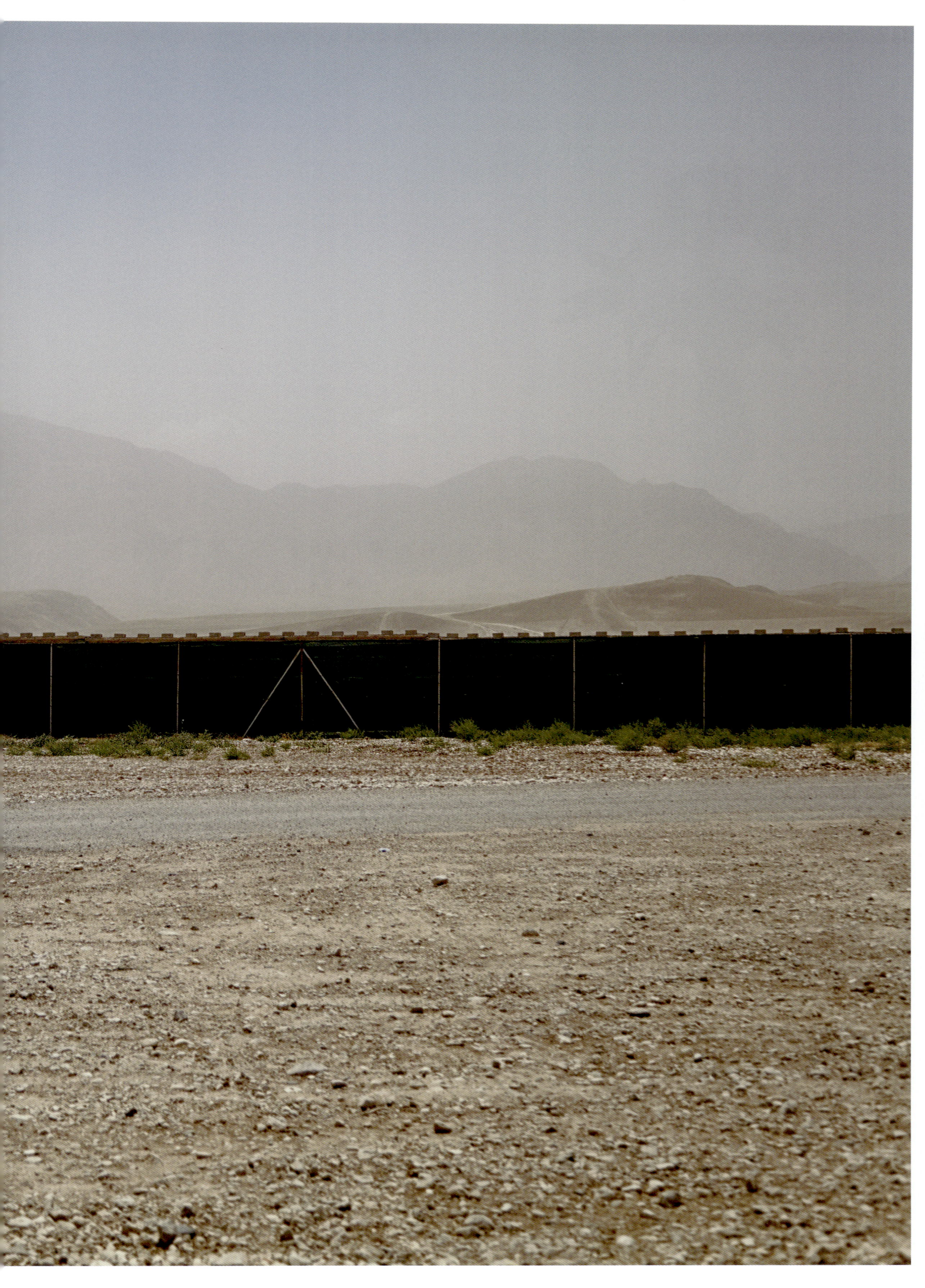

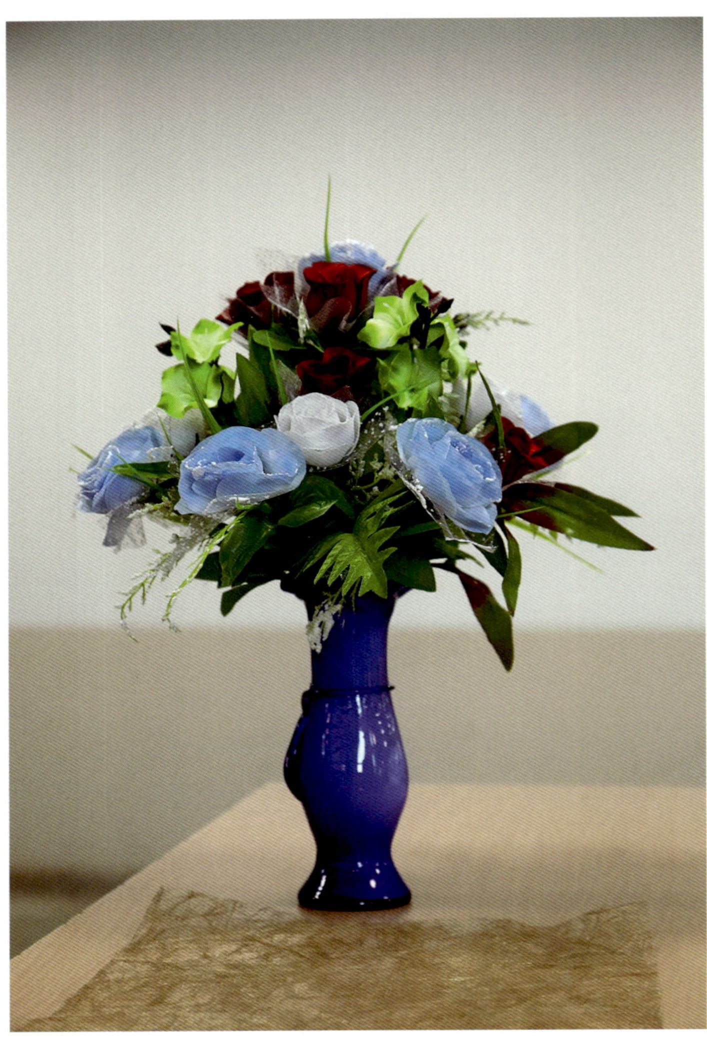

[16]

Beyond the barrier walls, the brown mountains lie in the sun. Inside the shipping container housing the training room, refrigerated beverages are available. The container itself is situated on the counter-I.E.D. training ground, which is meant to faithfully reproduce the landscape outside the barrier walls. There's a few hills, some shrubs, grass, dirt roads, a dried-up streambed, a couple of mud huts and burned-out vehicles. It's not entirely clear if the desolation in this landscape was deliberately recreated or has come about on its own accord. Inside the container is where Mr. K's "Low-Level" training takes place. He gives an account of the challenges he faces, which hardly differ from those of an instructor at any ordinary school. He has to maintain his students' attention, make them aware of certain things, effectively equip them with what they need to know, and so on. Only the terminology, also for personal conduct, is substantially more technical. Although Mr. K. insists there's some fun and games on the agenda, too.

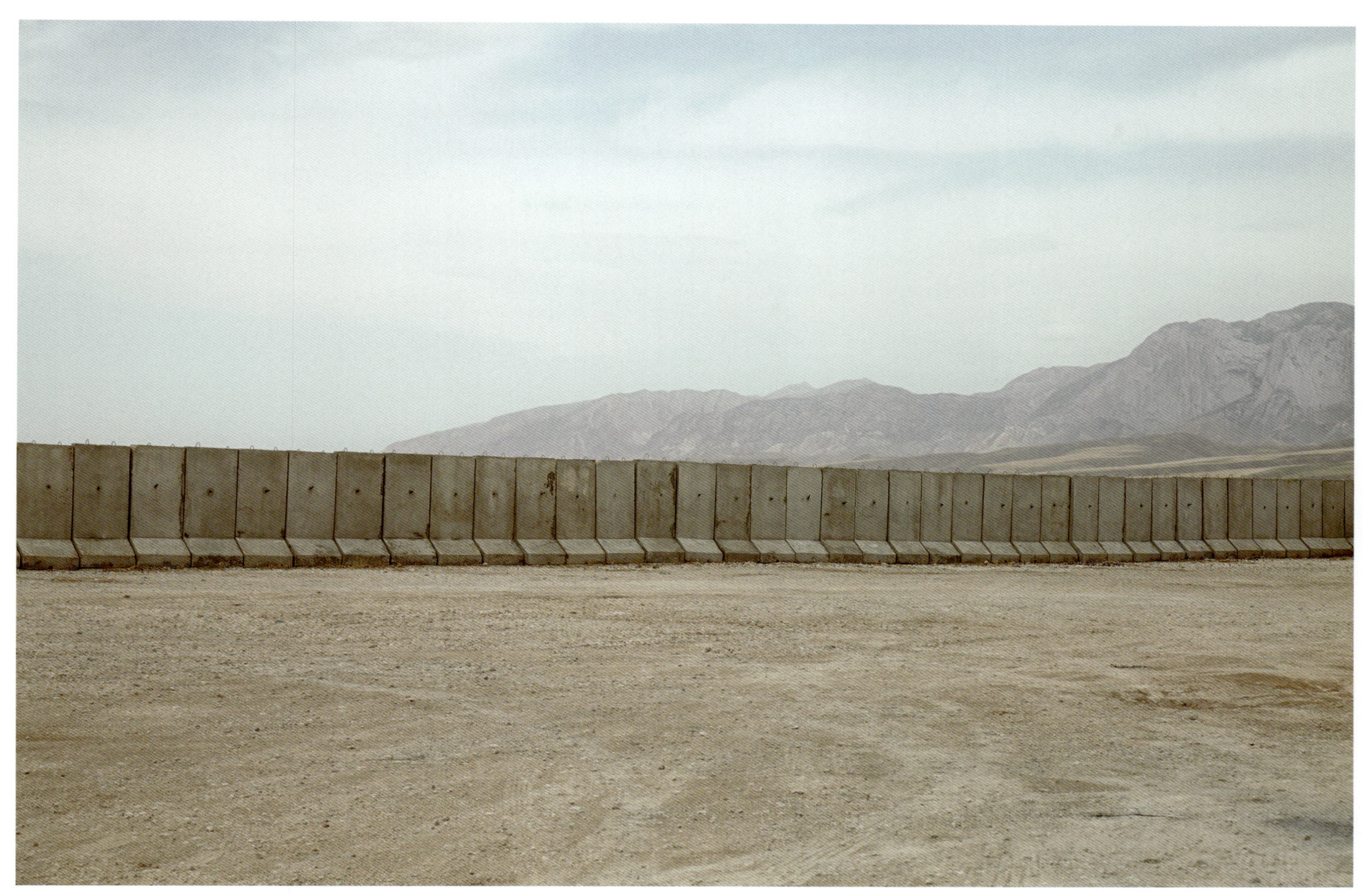

Located on the counter-I.E.D. training ground is a large hall in which improvised explosive devices have been reconstructed in mock-up form so as to simulate, for teaching purposes, how they were uncovered outside the camp, beyond the barrier walls. During a walk through the training course, Mr. K. poses a variety of didactic and leading questions. The most important part of his job, he reckons, is to impart to the others an awareness of their gut instinct. You have to be able to *sense* that something's not right.

[20]

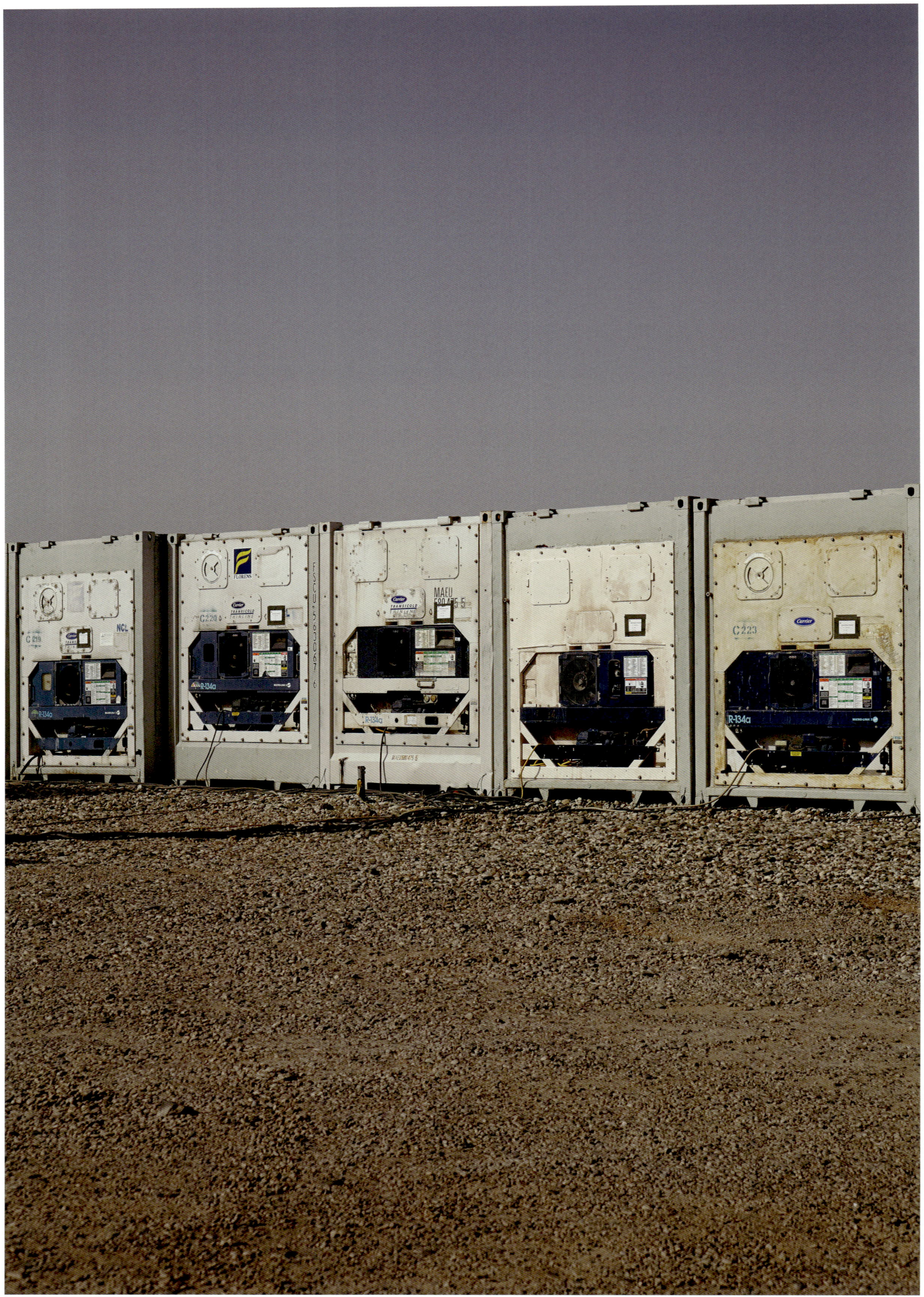

FLORENS
Carrier
TRANSICOLD
THINLINE
FSCU 58306? 6
Carrier
TRANSICOLD
MAEU
590.475 5
C 219
NCL
C 220
C 223
Carrier
R-134a
R-134a
R-134a
R-134a
MAEU 590.475 5
MICRO-LINK

An overwhelming majority of the soldiers will never leave
the confines of the camp. The impression they're able to
make for themselves of this country in which they're
stationed consists only of the view over the camp's walls
where the brown mountains and the black columns of
smoke from the waste incineration site lay beyond.
Apart from that, and aside from traversing the artificial
landscape of the counter-I.E.D. training ground, they
have only images: at morning briefings, on the internet,
in brochures and training videos. Certain scenarios from
the theater of war are reenacted on the counter-I.E.D.
training ground. Lieutenant Colonel S., responsible for
press and public relations, says: "Demonstration is the
best communication." The counter-I.E.D. training ground
thus doubles as a training ground for the battle of images.

[26]

[27]

An accident is reconstructed in which an all-terrain
vehicle under fire has driven into a drainage ditch. One of
the vehicle's two occupants has been hurt in the accident.
The other hauls his injured comrade out of the vehicle
and into a concrete shelter and calls for reinforcements.
Positioned on the surrounding mounds of earth are
high-ranking soldiers; they wear their berets against the
merciless sun and stand with their thumbs hooked into
their belt loops. Off to the side, additional observers sit at
the rear of a transport vehicle on long wooden folding
benches in the shade of a tarp stretched above them.
In the distance, the reinforcements approach from the edge
of the counter-I.E.D. training ground in a great cloud of
dust. The exercise is moderated in English by a German
soldier. He explains each step in the securing and recovery
of the vehicle. The injured soldier is being aided to in
the background, while in the fore, two minesweepers make
their way with garden rakes through the undergrowth.

As the only place in the camp not paved-over with
asphalt or gravel, the counter-I.E.D. training ground is
the preferred habitat of the Mongolian gerbil, which lives
in a symbiotic relationship with the sand fly, itself
a transmitter of the particularly treatment-resistant
infectious disease leishmaniasis.

This simulated environment recreated in the camp
is sufficiently authentic for these critters to make it their
home.

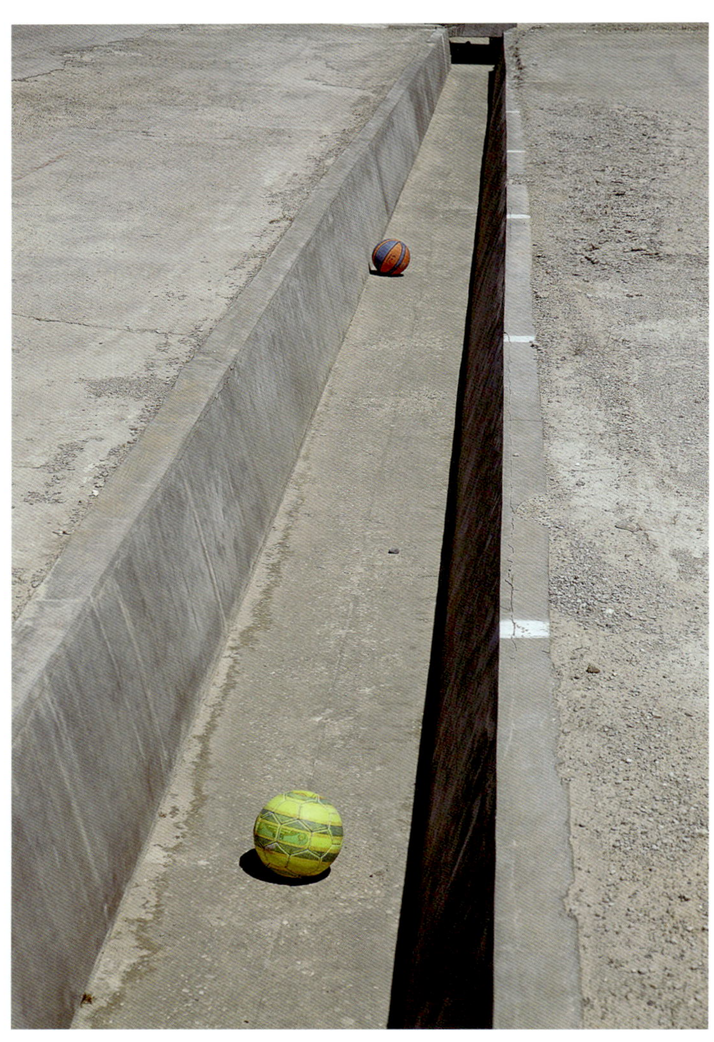

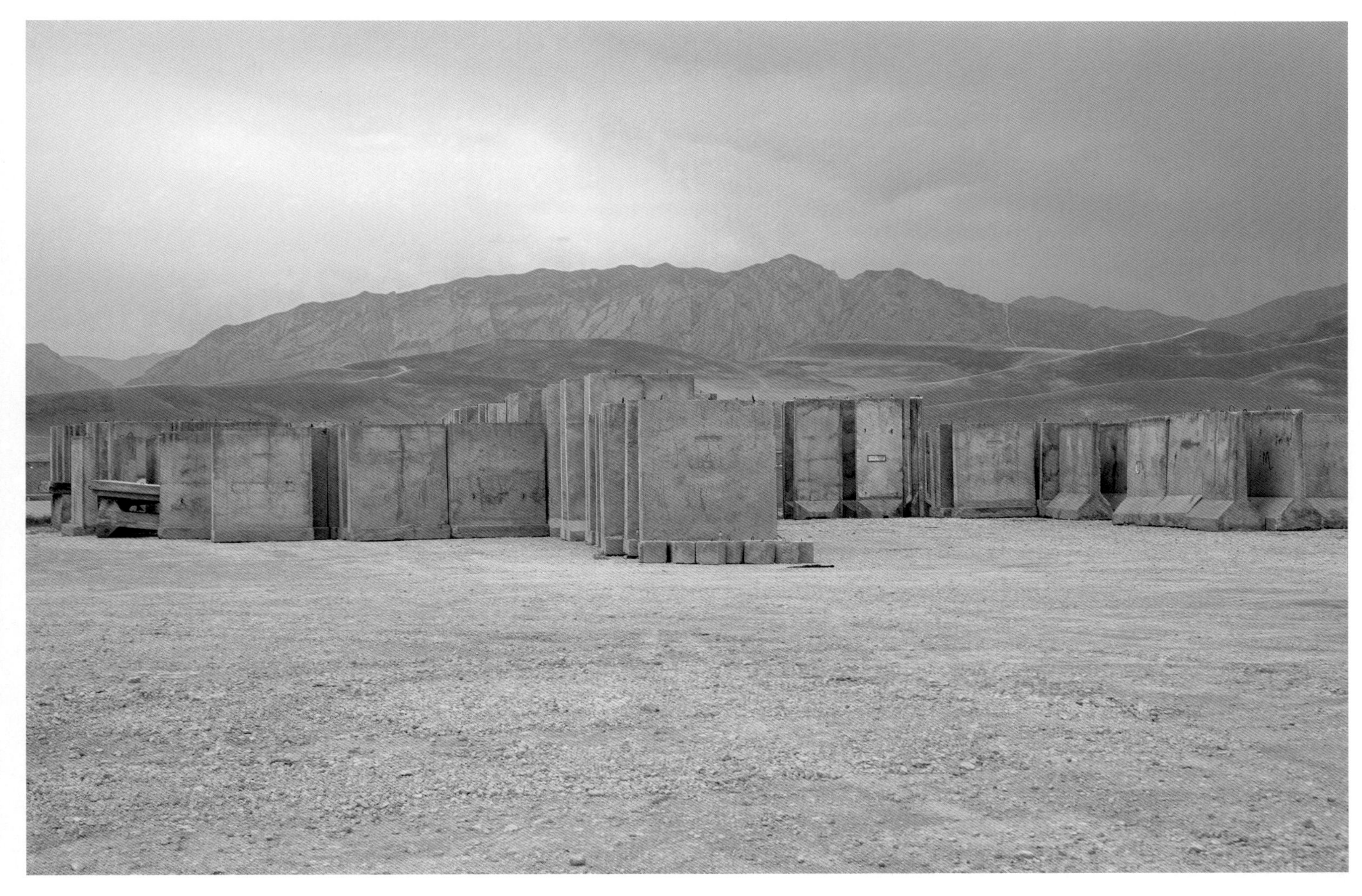

[35]   [36]

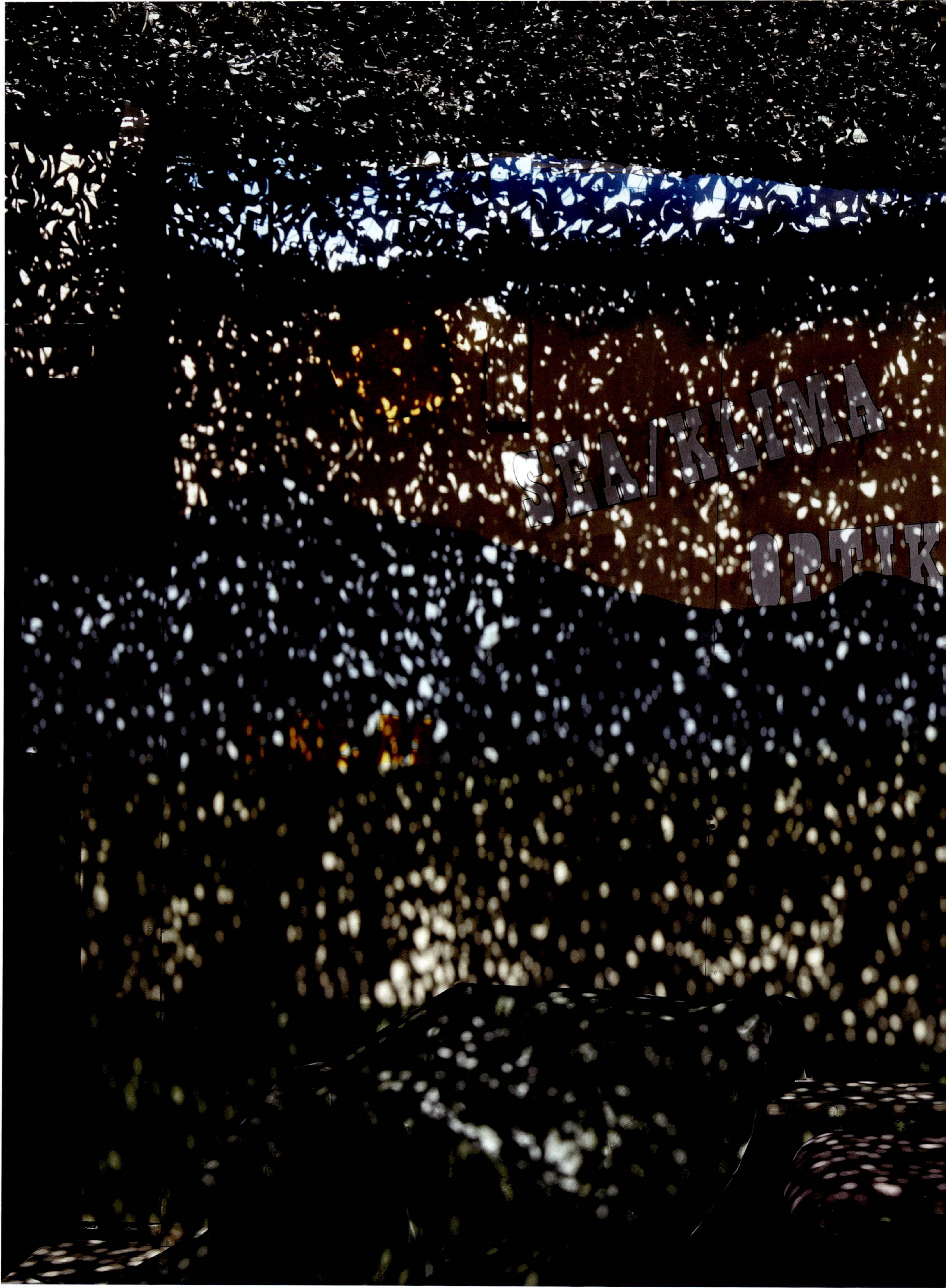
SEA/KLIMA
OPTIK

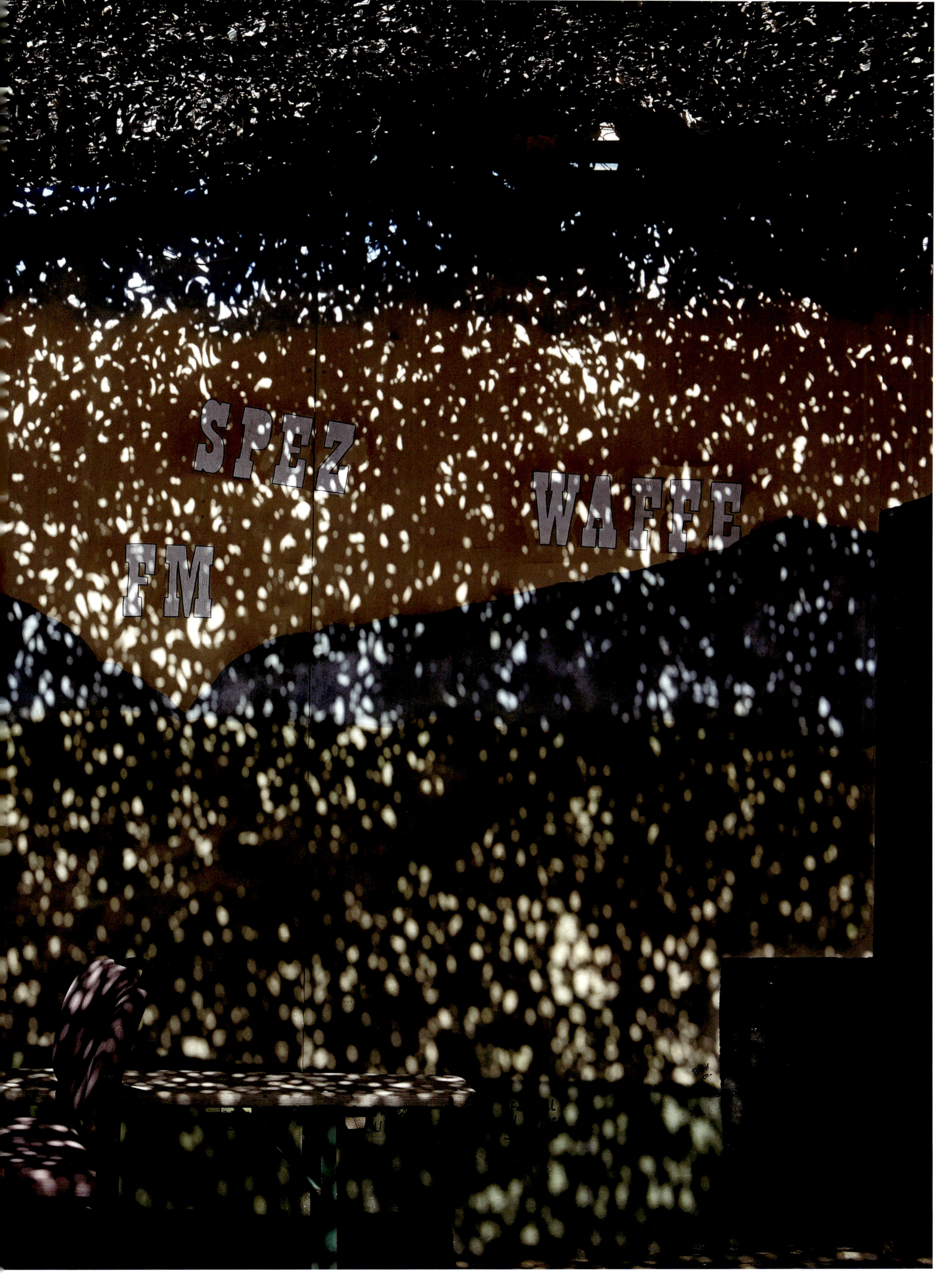
SPEZ
FM
WAFFE

[53]

[54]

[55]

[56]

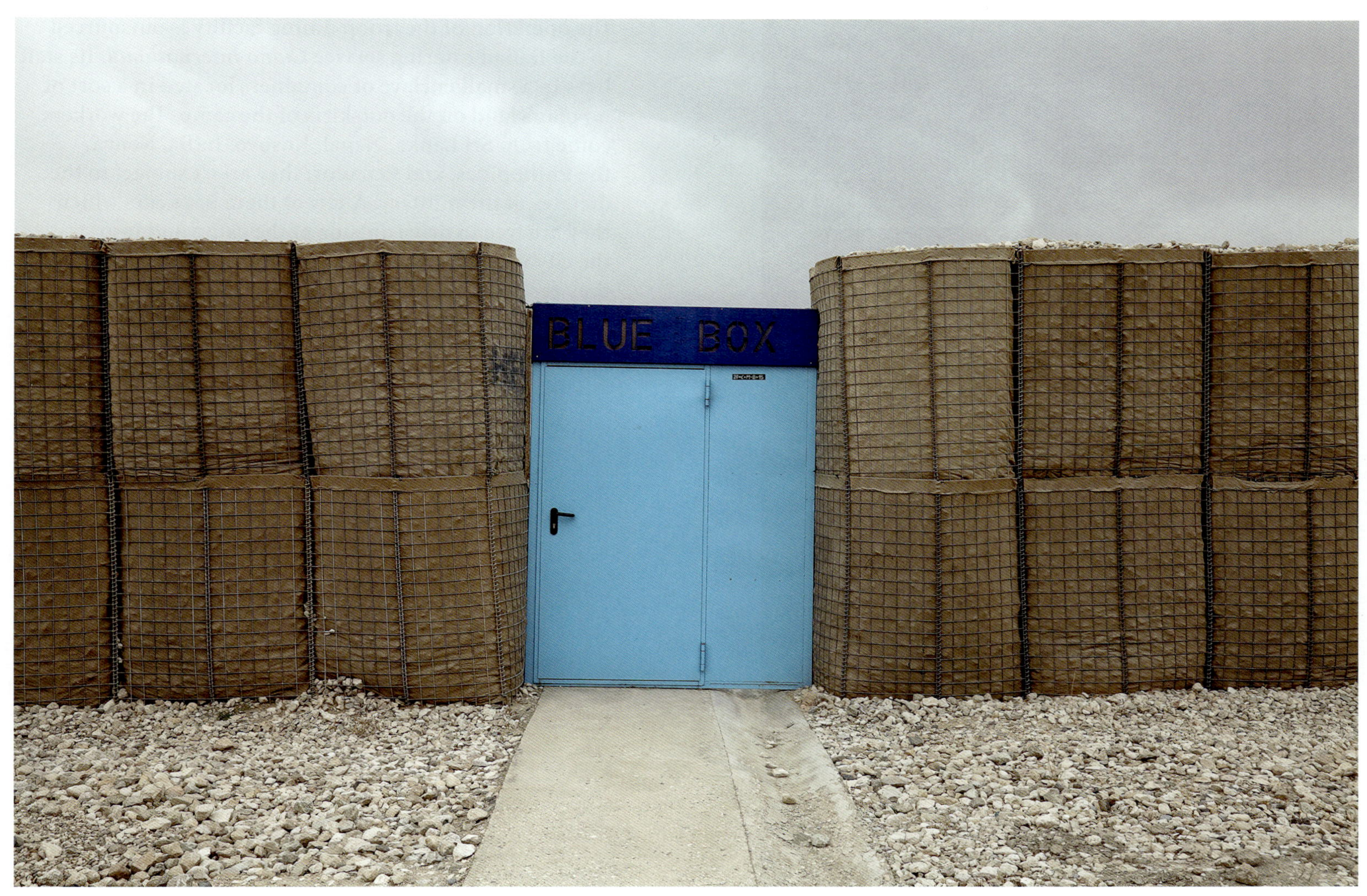

A dust storm rises up and shrouds the camp in a surreal, beige-colored curtain of light. The wind whistles and howls along the buildings, and from all possible places, the memorial for fallen soldiers, there comes an underworldly wailing, and with it a high metallic clanking from the flag poles. At some point even the reconnaissance balloon is brought in, as nothing can be seen now anyway. This evening in the Atrium's 'Oase', as on every Monday night at eight o'clock, there's a film showing. Tonight it's *I Am Number Four*—an American high school fantasy movie about aliens who are visually indistinguishable from human beings and are hiding out on Earth from other aliens. In the film, the other aliens have already wiped out the entire population of those who are hiding from them, with the exception of the remaining nine, who they are now hunting down systematically on Earth. The aliens who look like humans and are on the run can only be killed by the others in a particular order (it is not explained why this is). The film tells the story of the fourth alien in line, who falls in love with a beautiful photographer, discovers he has super powers, and decides to stop running away and face his enemies.

[60]

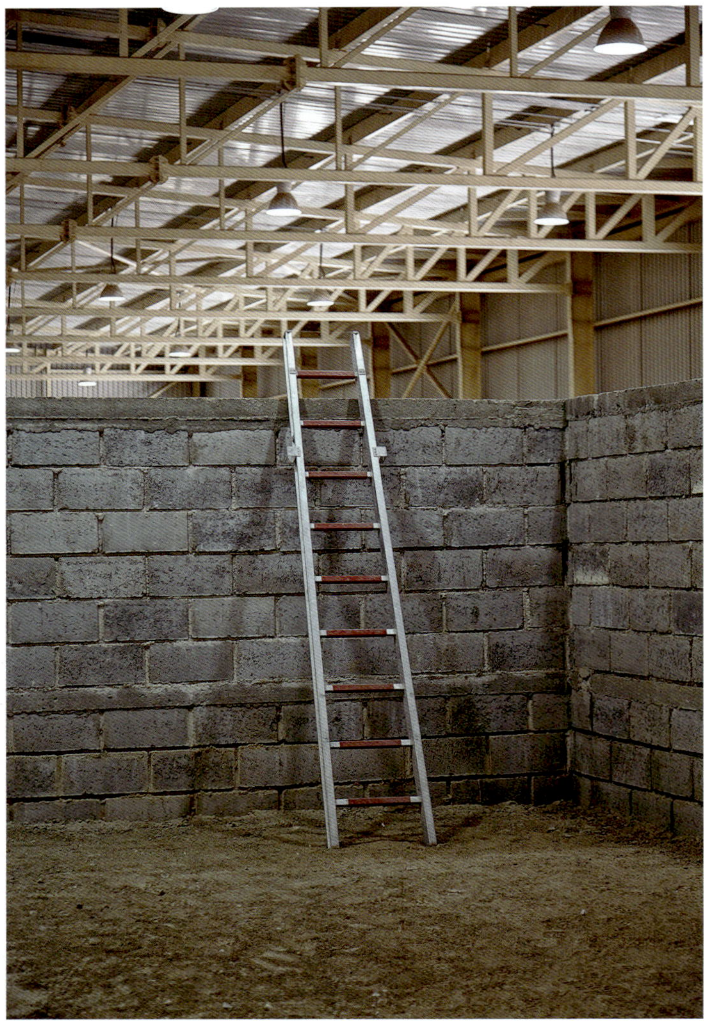

The operation of the troop dining facility is outsourced to the Italian catering service *Ciano International*. Its staff lives in a small enclave of containers located in a sort of no man's land on the outskirts of the camp. The workers come from Sri Lanka, Nepal, Kosovo, India, Kenya, the Philippines, and Ecuador; they aren't subject to the dictates of the military. A few of them have cars which they are free to drive outside of the camp and into the city whenever they like. Beyond the camp's borders, they receive no escort and are not armed.

It isn't the assortment of little makeshift soldier-run bars servicing virtually all areas of military operation not already covered by the Atrium's official support facilities, but arguably this container community of dining facility personnel that embodies the true subculture of the camp.

[64]

The manager of the dining facility is from Germany and has worked in the camp for eleven years. Germany, he says, reflecting on his most recent attempt to return home, is a place he just can't stand anymore. In the dining facility itself stand long rows of tables adjacent to one another at which the soldiers from the various nations sit and eat. With sufficient practice, walking past the rows of backs bent over plates, one comes to recognize the respective nationality of each uniform by various designs on their fatigues. The widely diverse patterns on the uniforms offer a variety of interpretations of the desert's dust and scrub. The uniforms are treated with an insect repellent which, with frequent laundering, lends a faint pink tinge to the fabric. One can pick out the veterans by this rosy tinge, at least the ones who seldom request new uniforms.

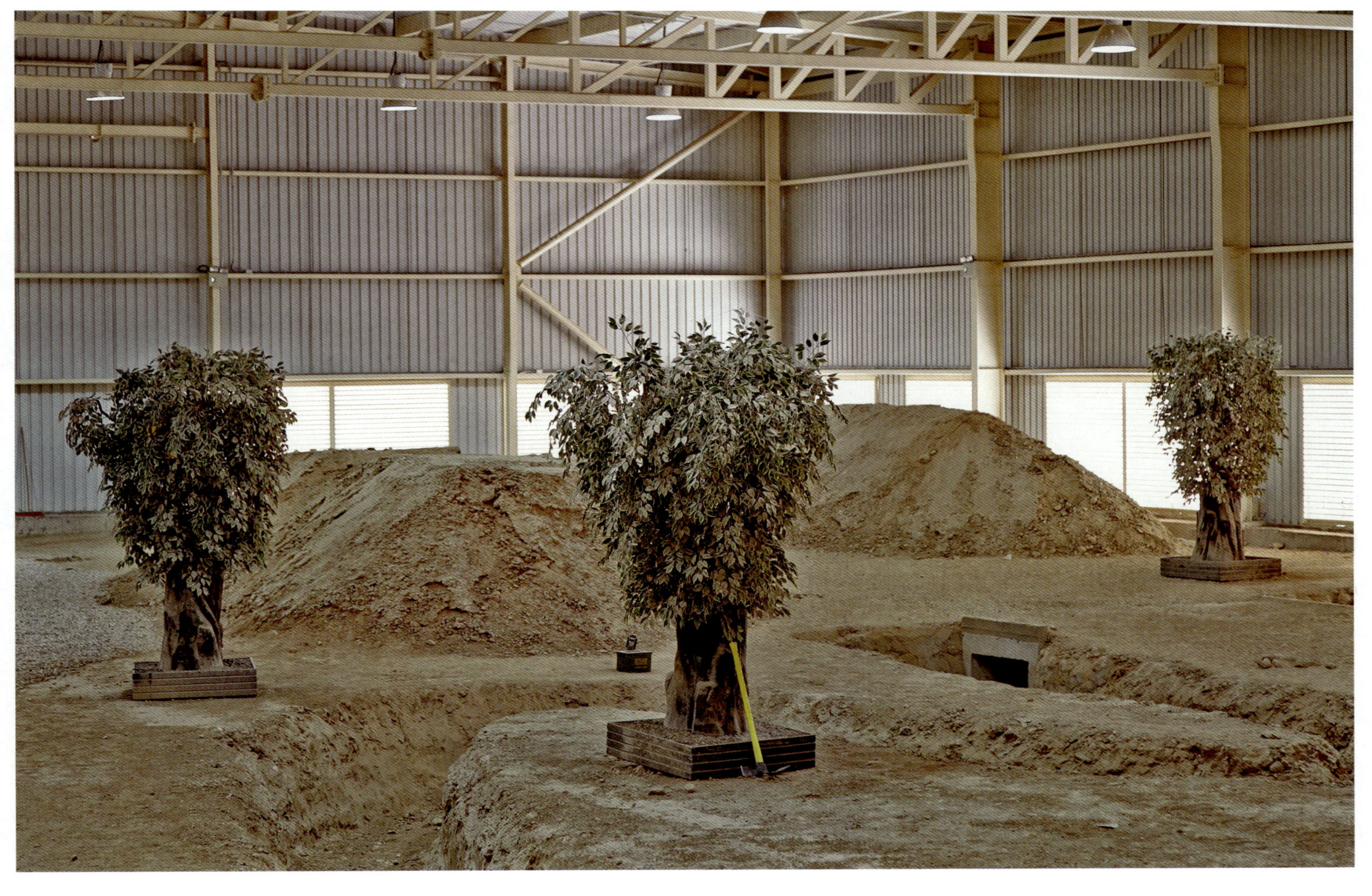

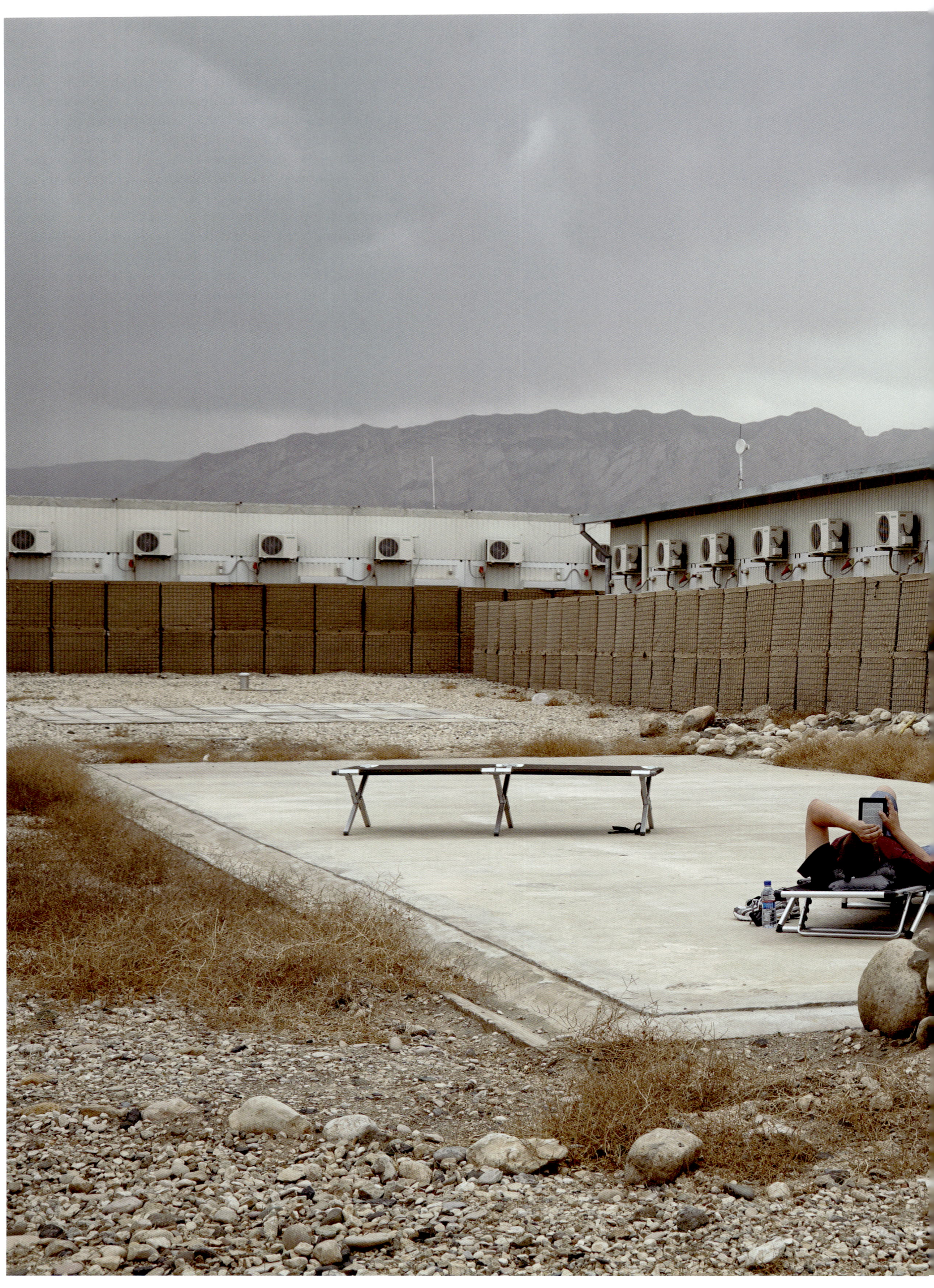

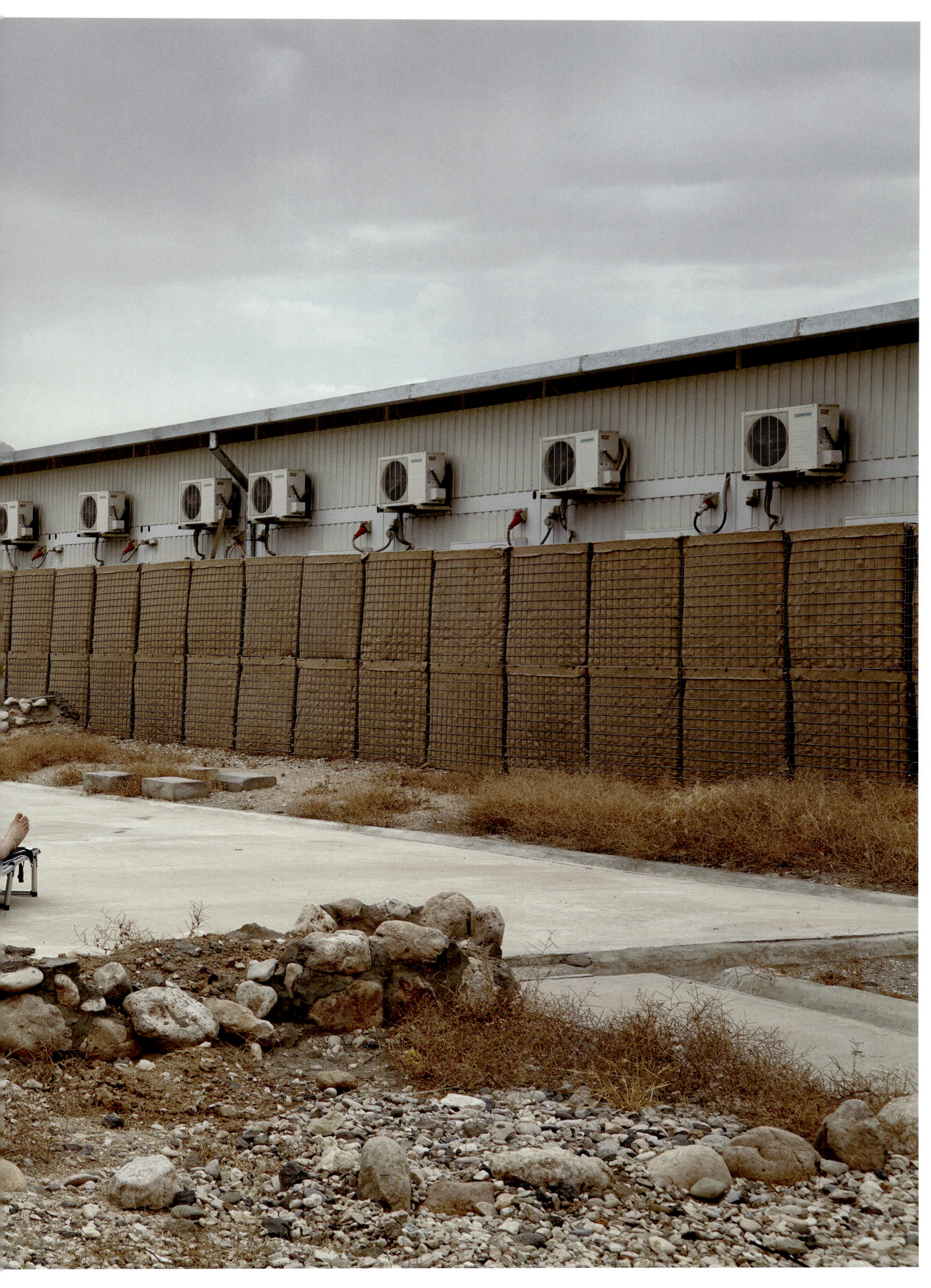

Of the camp's former American sector, only the foundations remain. A broad expanse of concrete slabs in the ground. Here and there they bear traces that indicate the nature of the purpose they once served. On one of the slabs, the lines of a gymnasium's basketball court are still visible.

[81]

[82]

[83]

[84]

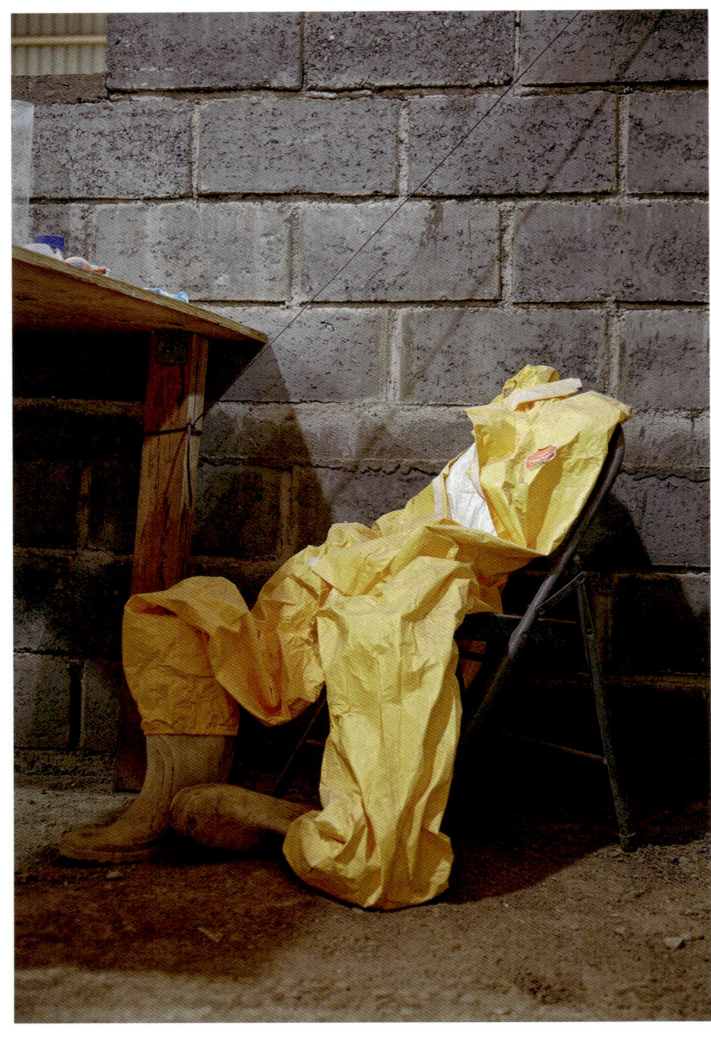

[87]

The American contingent had lived in tents that were erected on the concrete foundations and have since been completely dismantled and removed. Next to each foundation, there sits a small concrete shelter ready in case of an airstrike.

Theater of War: "An area or place in which important military events occur or are progressing. The Theater of War can include the entirety of the air space, land and sea area that is or that may potentially become involved in war operations."

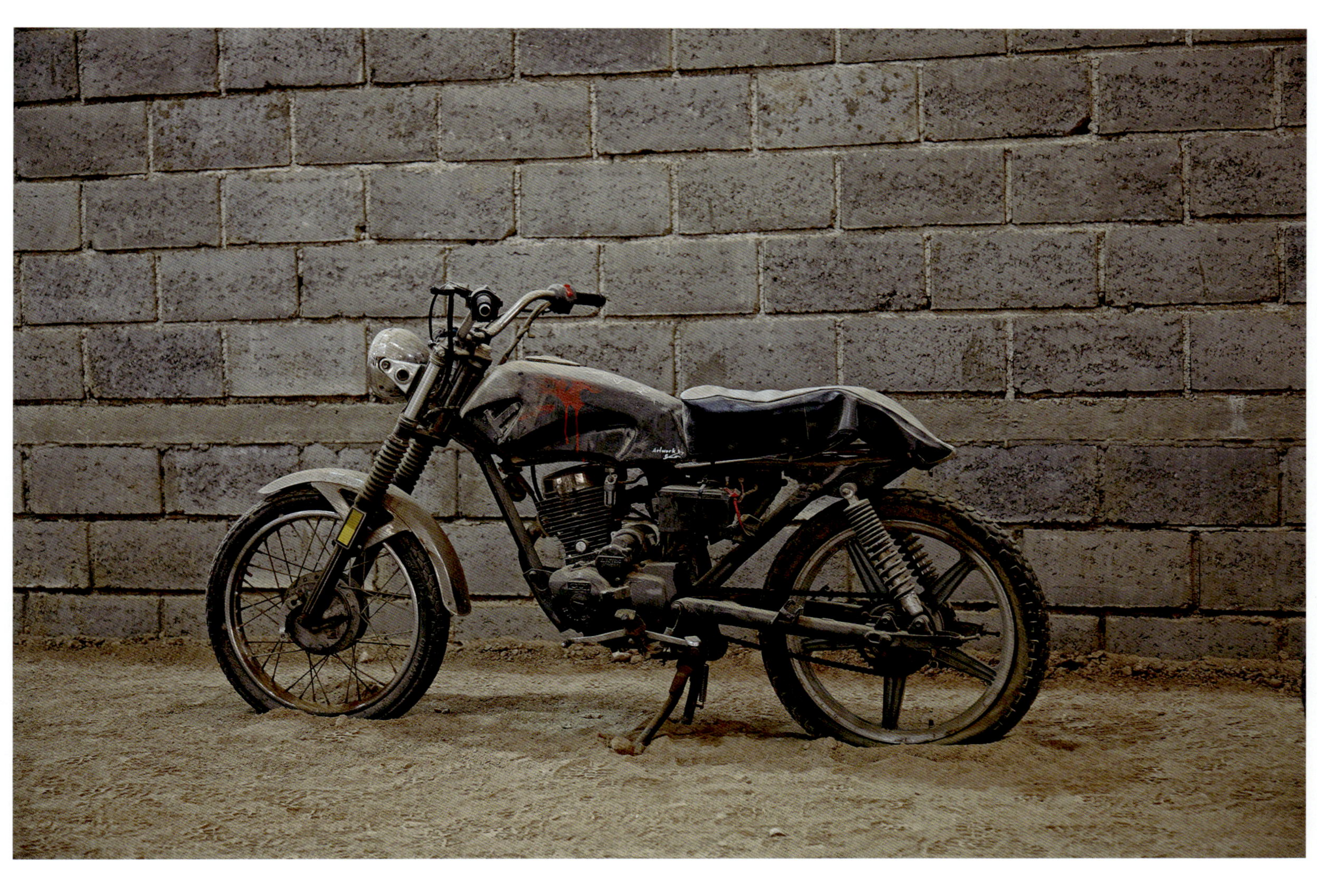

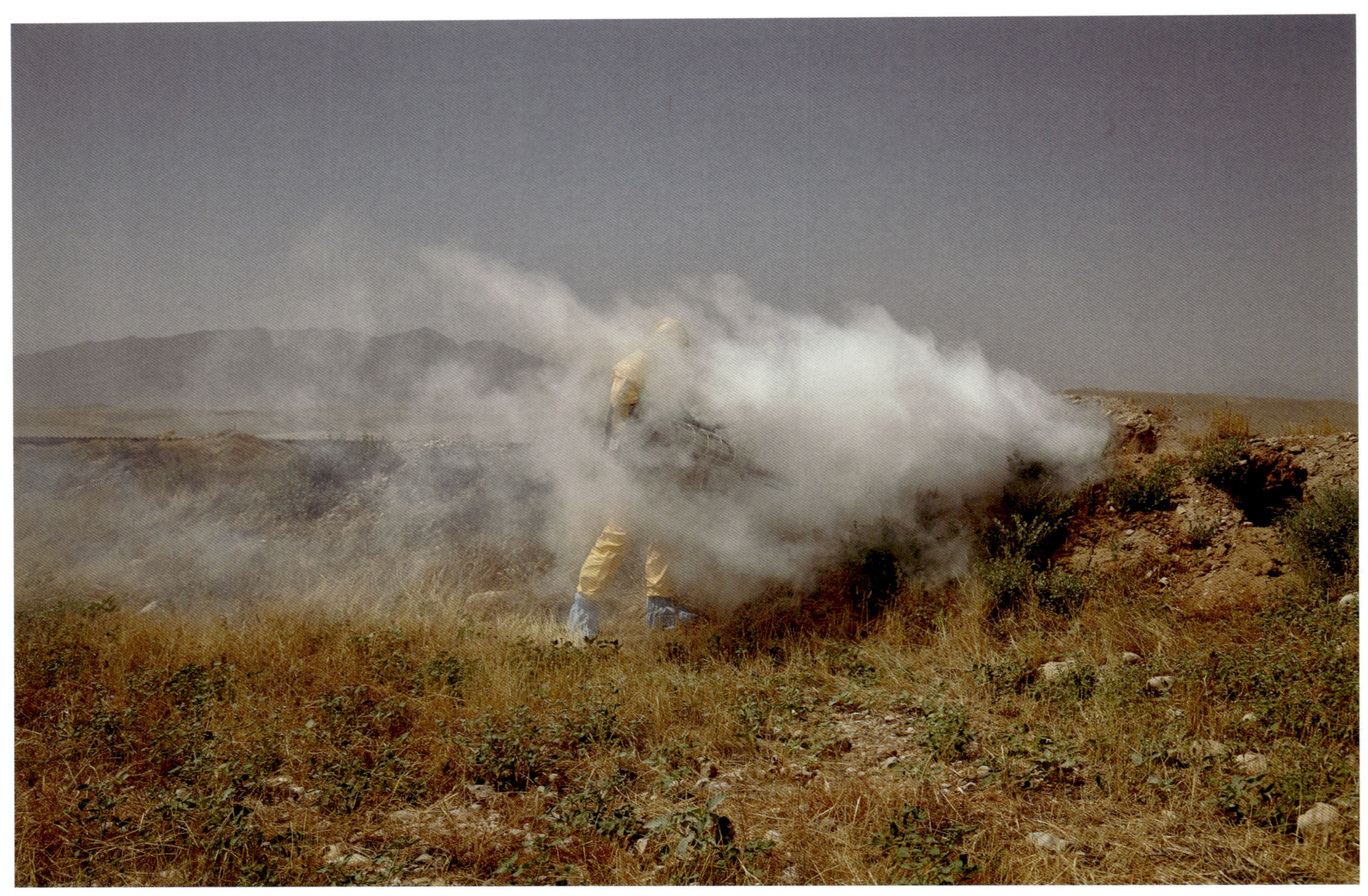

Inside the yurt of the Mongolian Commander, soldiers
are seated on two pieces of bed-like furniture against the
wall. There's a shrine for the god of war Ulaan Jamsaran,
a Genghis Khan wall hanging, and 34 laminated depic-
tions of other Mongolian emperors. On a flat-screen tele-
vision, a documentary is playing about Mongolia from
the Austrian Broadcasting Corporation.
One of the soldiers seated on the bed-like furniture is asked
to demonstrate traditional Mongolian throat singing
dating back to the time of Manduul Khan and a 500-year-
old welcoming ceremony. The air is too dry, though,
and too dusty for the singing soldier, his performance
interrupted constantly by his need to cough, and eventually
abandoned altogether as it simply isn't working.

[96]

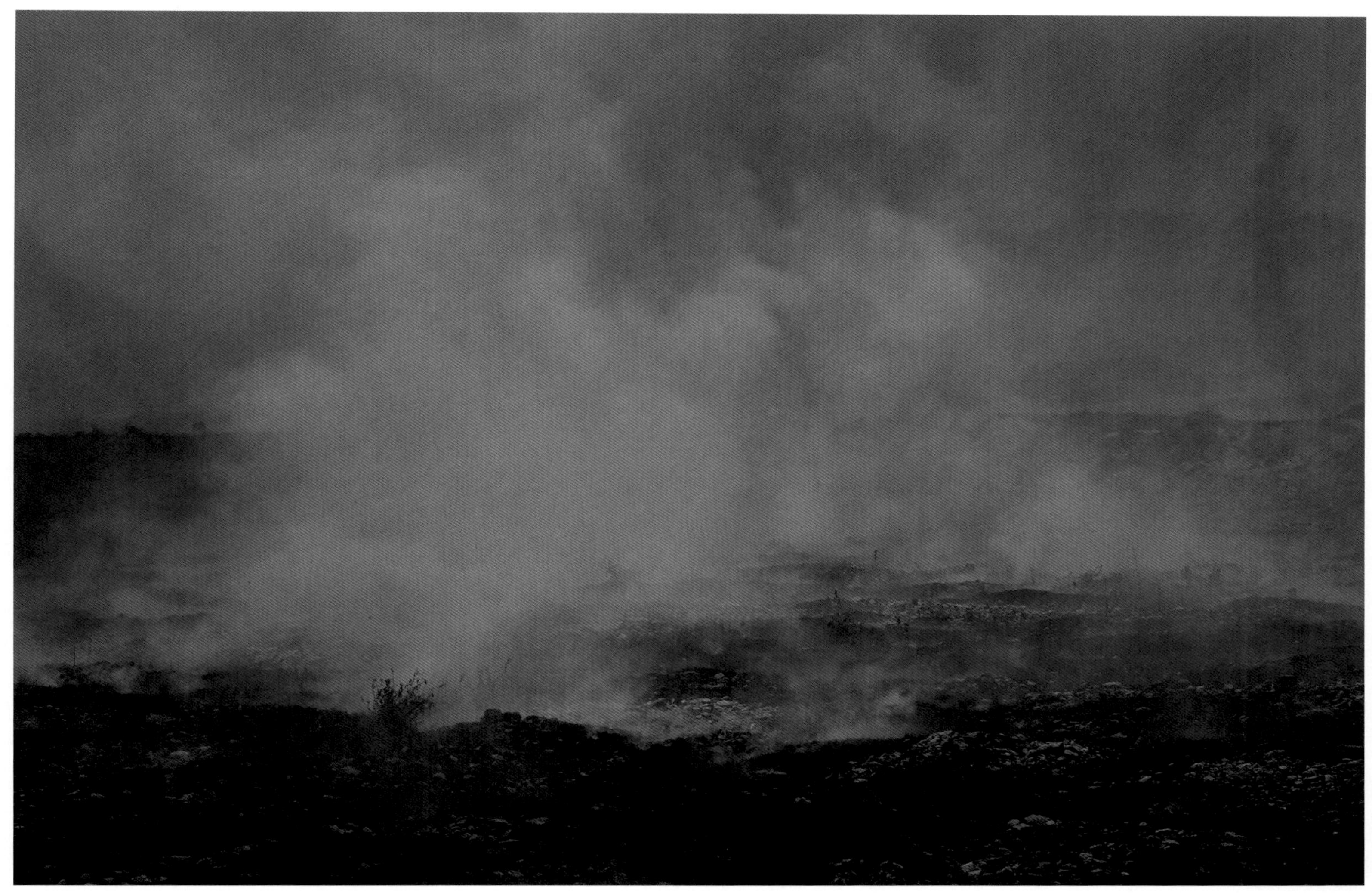

In lieu of the live performance, a video clip is shown
on the flat-screen TV in which a professional Mongolian
throat singer appears in traditional garb on Germany's
competitive singing reality show, *Deutschland sucht
den Superstar*, and performs for Dieter Bohlen the melody
from "Cheri, Cheri Lady" using his special technique.
Afterwards there's a promotional film about Mongolia,
consisting primarily of aerial photography of Ulaanbaatar,
and a kind of music video that the press officer has put
together about the contingent and his time in the camp.
When it comes time to leave, each visitor is given a Mongolian Ministry of Defense coin as a souvenir.

[100]

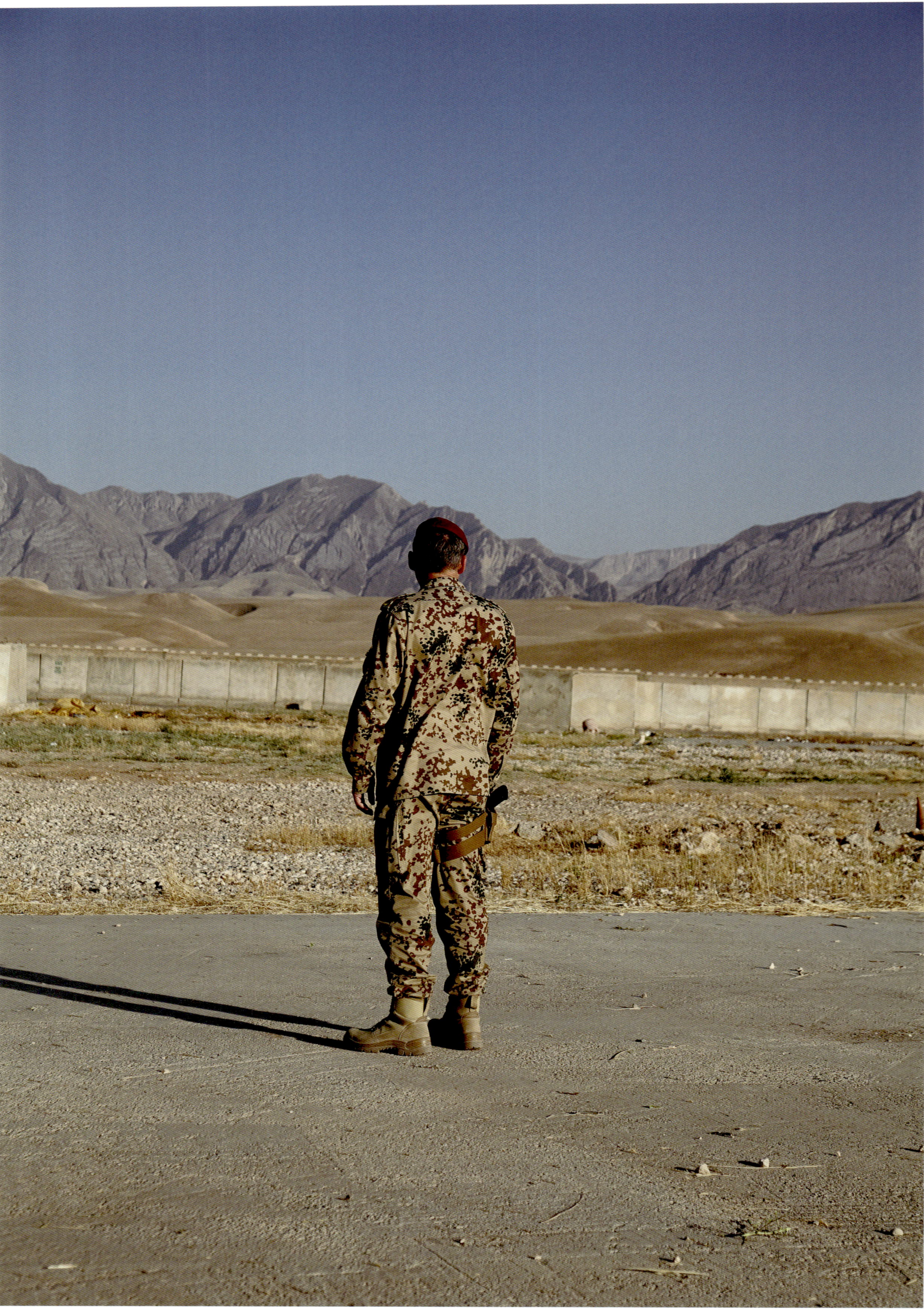

[105]

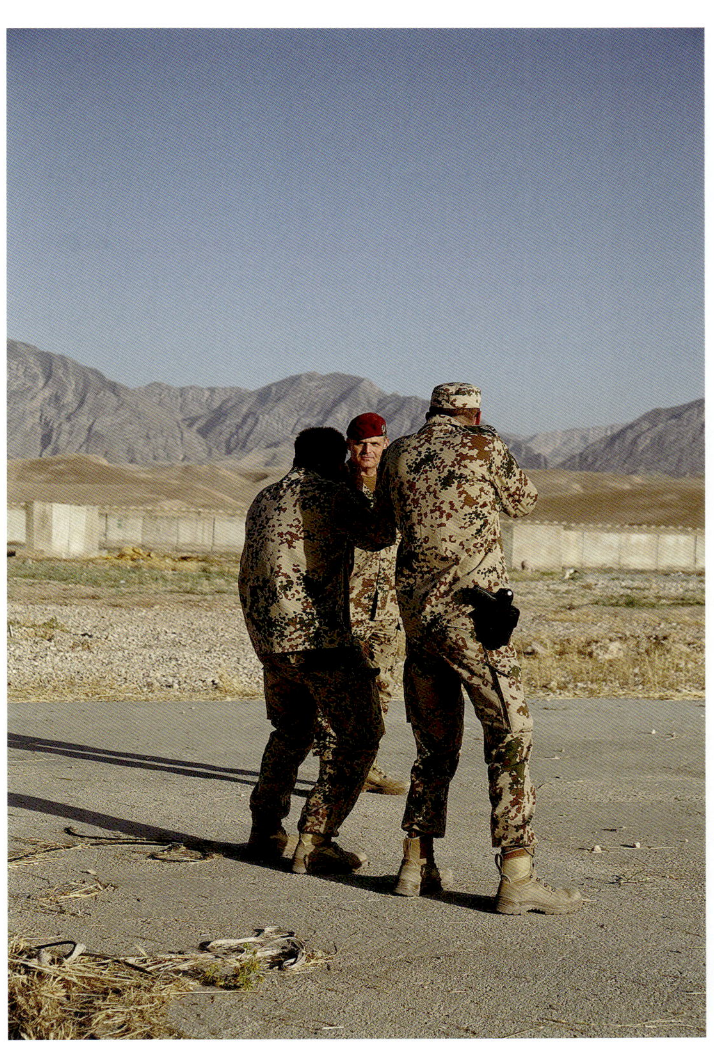

[107]

[108]

Tasked with providing camp security and trained in advance in Germany, the Armenian troops have constructed a church for themselves on camp grounds. This is already the second one to be built on the same spot. The first church had been made of wood, and burned to the ground a few years ago. Two charred wooden panels on the brick walls of the new church bear witness to this. A plaque is mounted outside which reads: "Fire can burn the walls, but there is no force in the world that could destroy our religion and love for God."

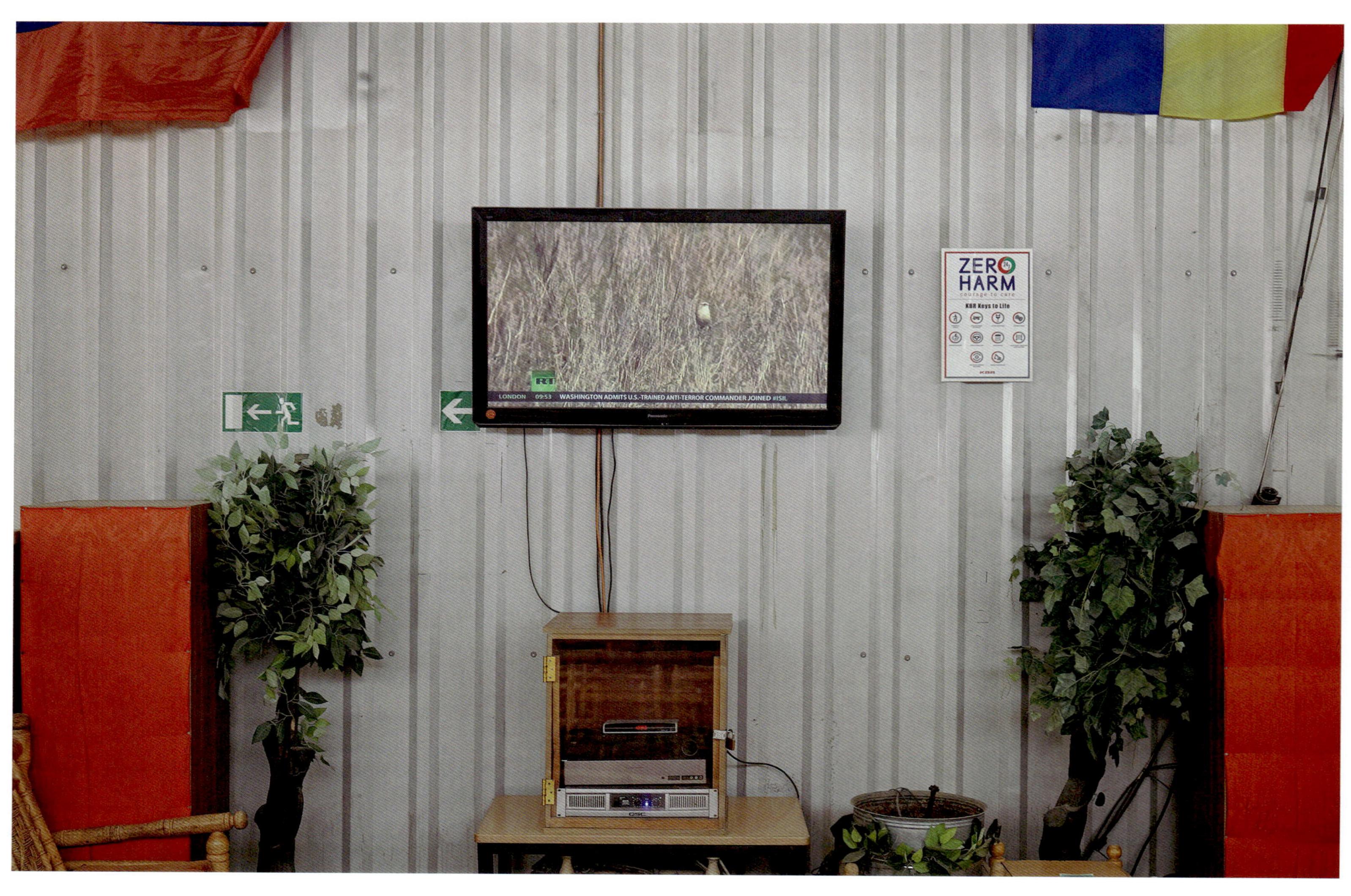

The images of the saints in the church as well as the murals
painted on the walls of the container vestibule to the
Armenian commandant's office are all without exception
the work of the soldiers. On one wall hang a collection of
flags and an explanatory notice behind transparent plastic:
these are the nations that have recognized the Armenian
Genocide. The German flag has already been added.

[116]

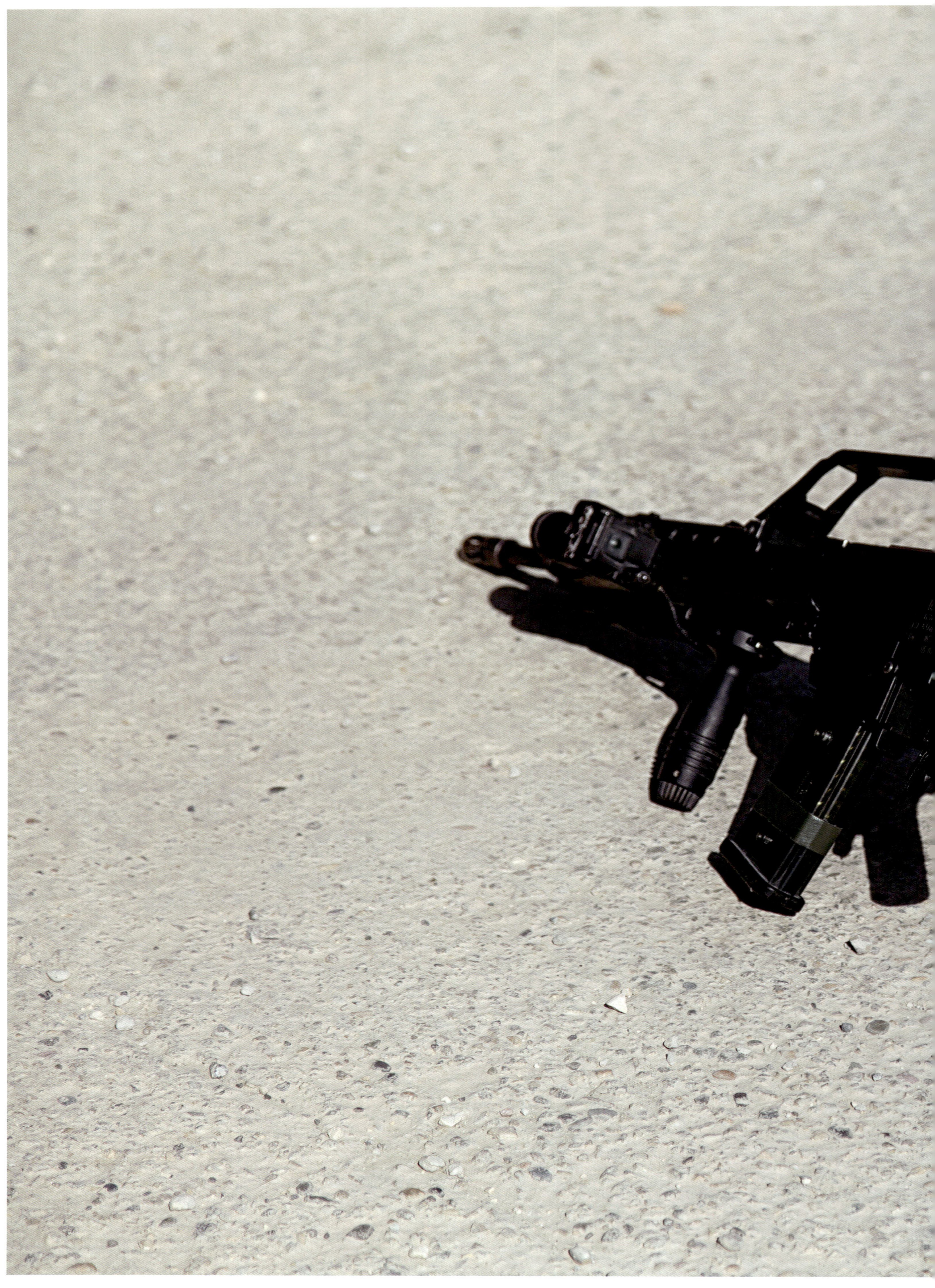

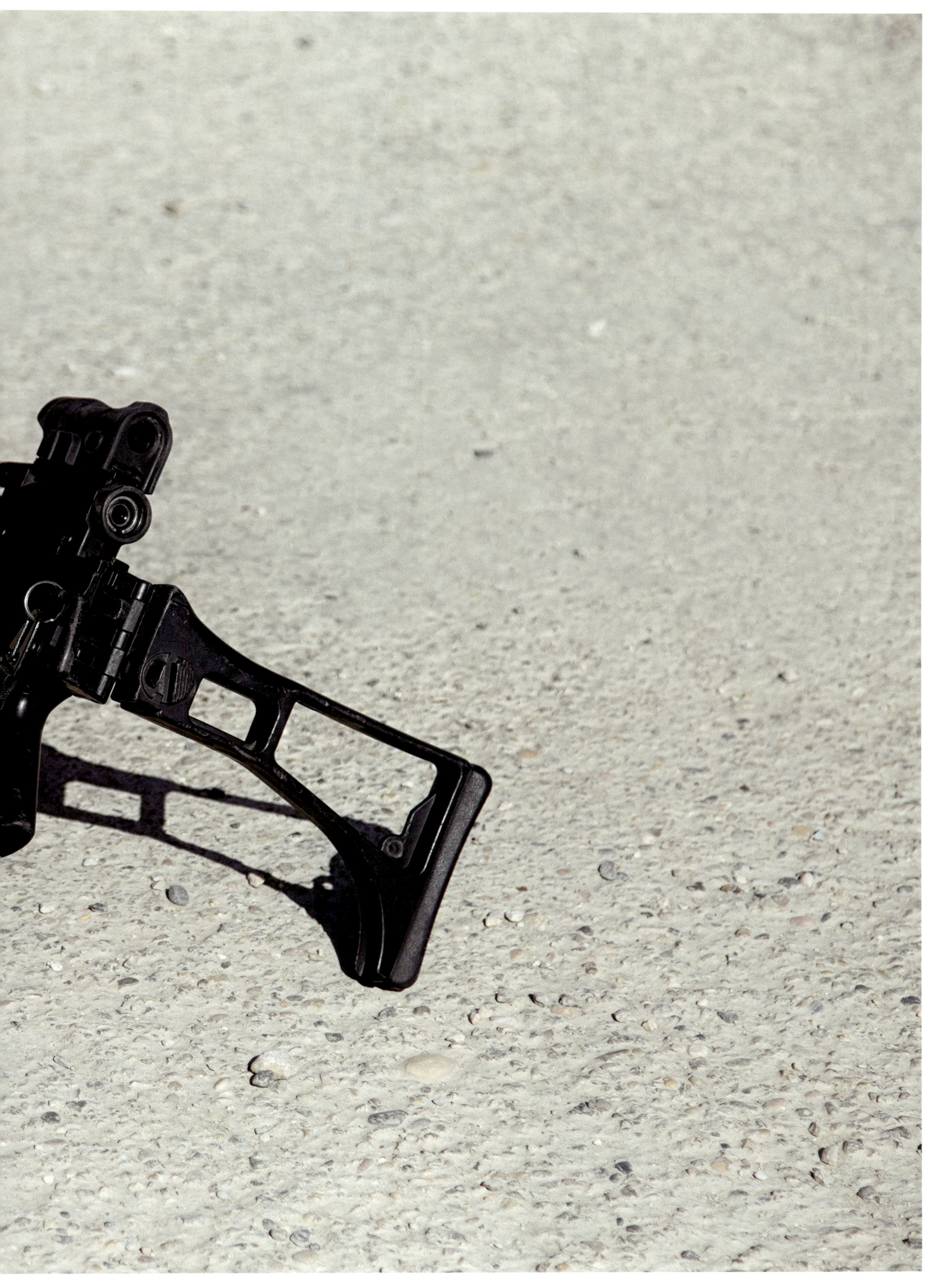

In addition to the Armenian church, the camp has a prayer room available for Muslims as well as a Christian chapel, which is led in alternating months by either an evangelical or catholic clergy.

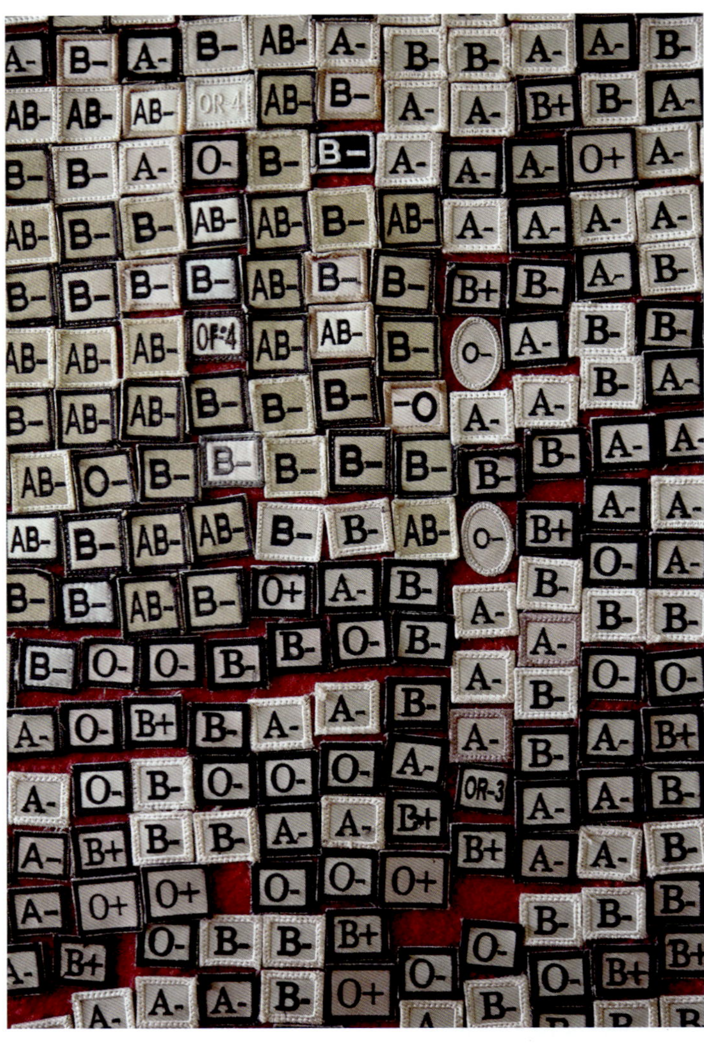

[128]

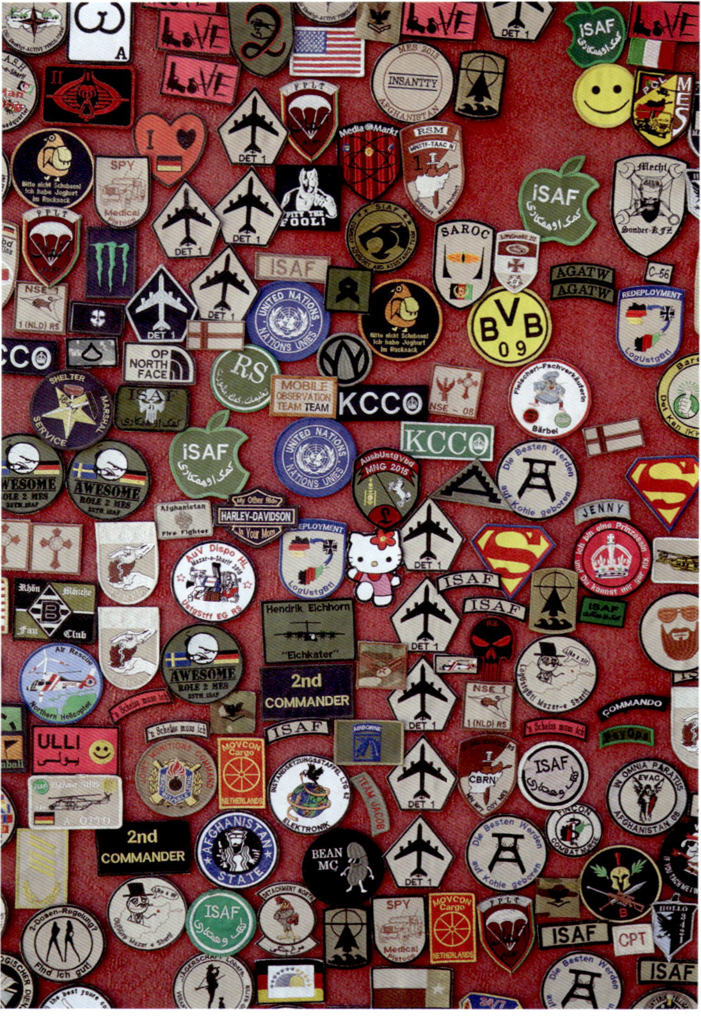

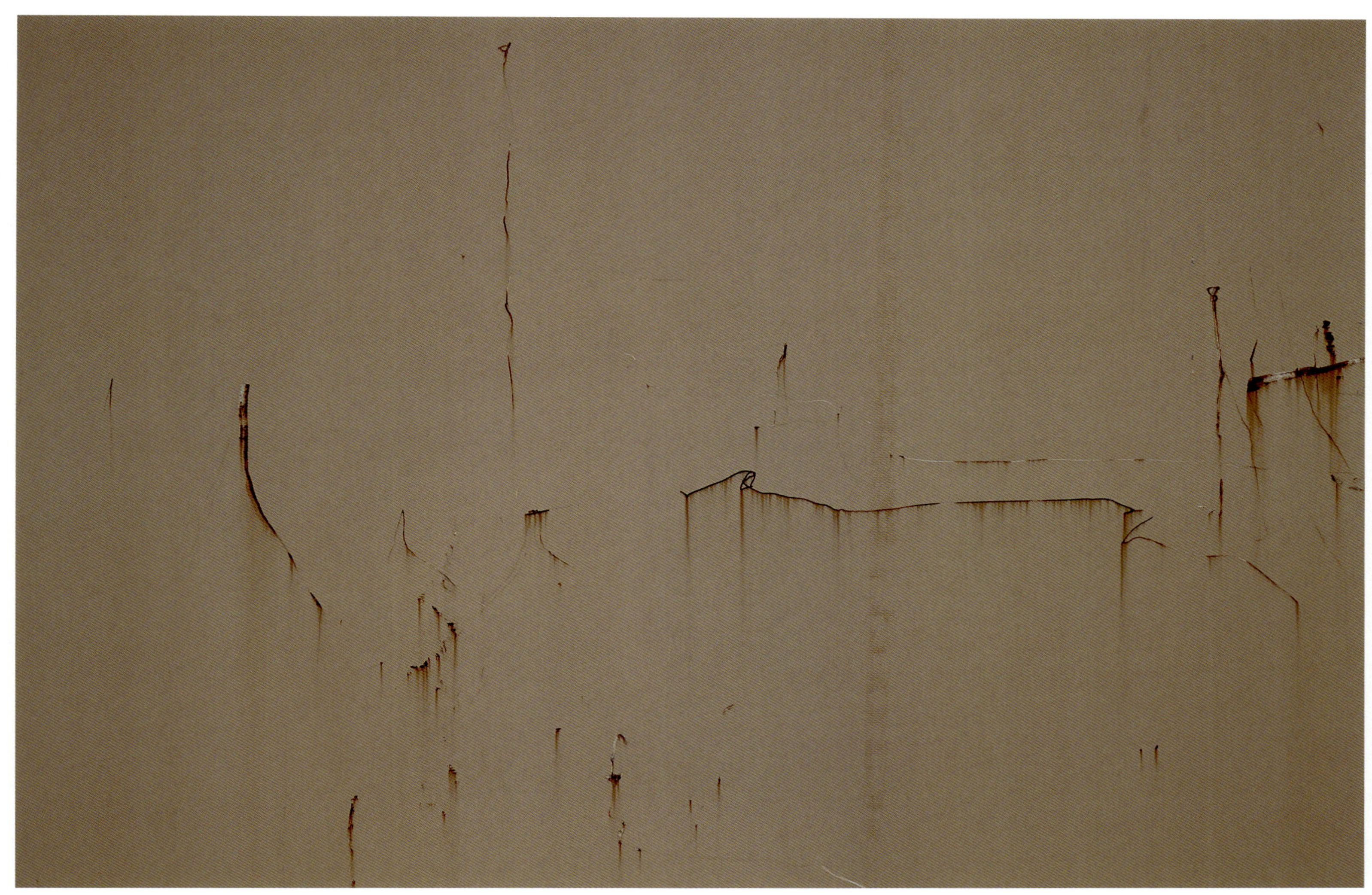

Already at the airbase in Cologne, the number of
military-specific publications from Christian organizations
available in the newspaper stands and magazine racks
had been striking. It would probably be wrong to conclude,
however, that these church-based institutions were
trying to recruit new members here among the soldiers.
Far more obvious would be the supposition that there
exists between the Army and the Church an indisputable
structural relationship: in their foundational principles of
faith and trust, their collective compliance with the
commands of a higher power, their suggestion that one
can die *for a cause*, or at least under the comforting illu-
sion that one's death will not be meaningless, in the security
of being in a group that transcends all individuality,
and in their belief in planting the vision of a better
world in this one not yet redeemed, as one plants a seed
in a garden.

[132]

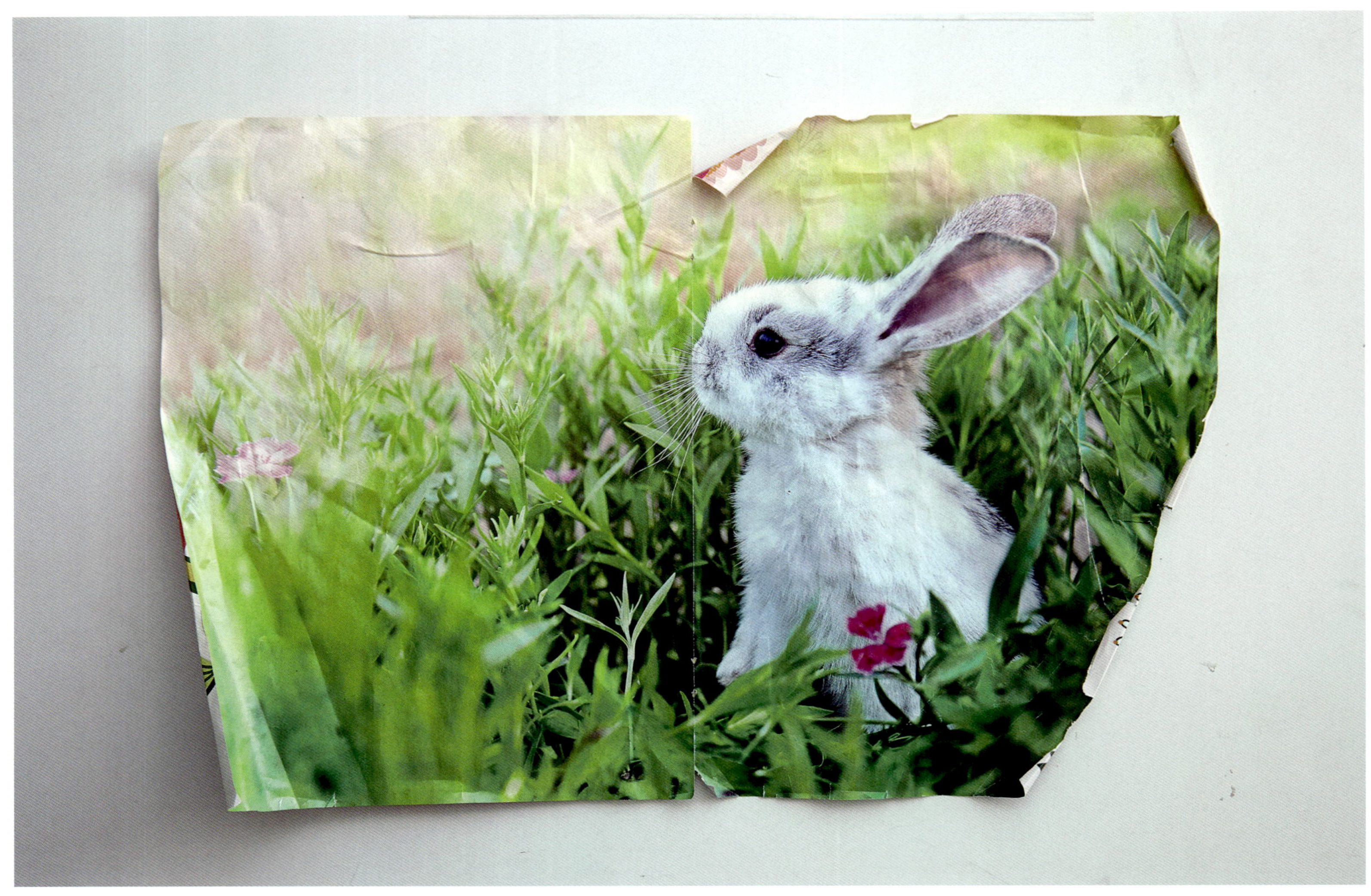

[135]

The divine gardener in the garden of human souls:
"Salvation has come into this heart today and I shall no
longer dwell on its misdeeds. I shall restore what
was destroyed, lift up what has fallen, and make fast that
which has come undone."

[137]

[138]

[139]

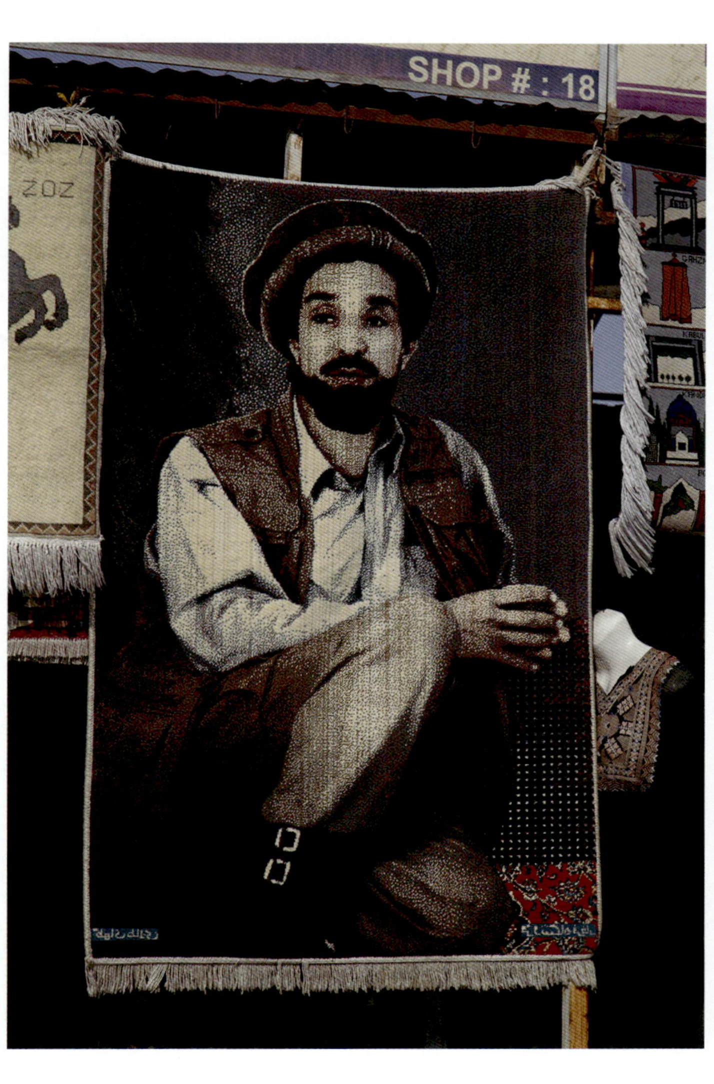

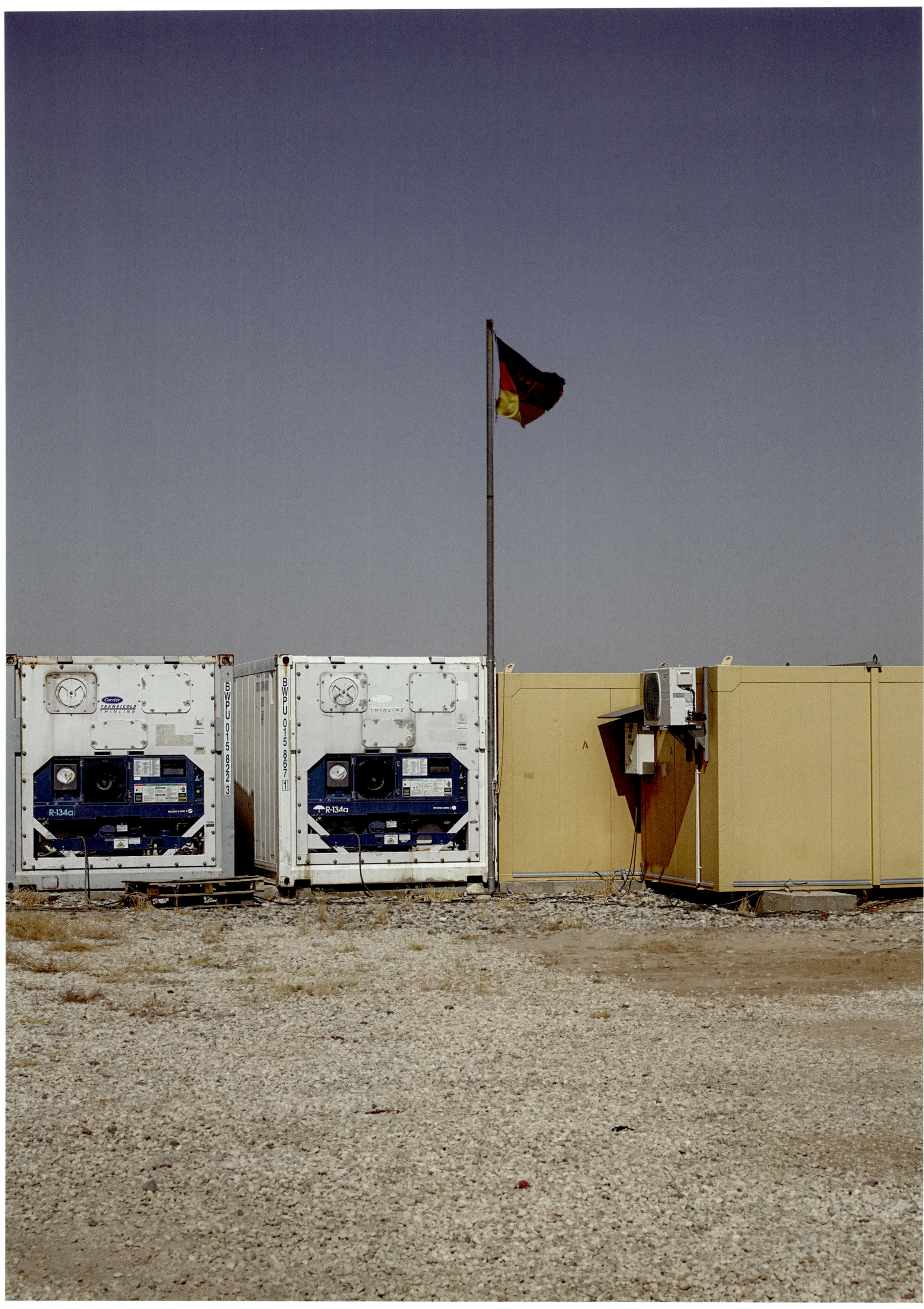

Carrier
TRANSICOLD
THINLINE
BWPU 015 822 3
R-134a
THINLINE
BWPU 015 897 1
R-134a
A

Laundry bag,
Please check all that apply:

Sun hat
Field blouse
Combat trousers
Combat jacket
Jacket liner
Undershirt, brown
Underpants, brown
Undershirt, thermal
Undershirt, long
Undershirt, turtleneck, green
Undershirt, olive
Jogging shorts
Socks, white
Towel
Sport jersey
Training jacket
Handkerchief
Tank suit
Socks, brown
Socks, olive
Field cap
Bed sheets
Duvet cover
Pillowcase
Coverall
T-shirt
Panties/Underpants

Pajamas
Skirt
Lingerie bag
Scarf
Gloves
Mask

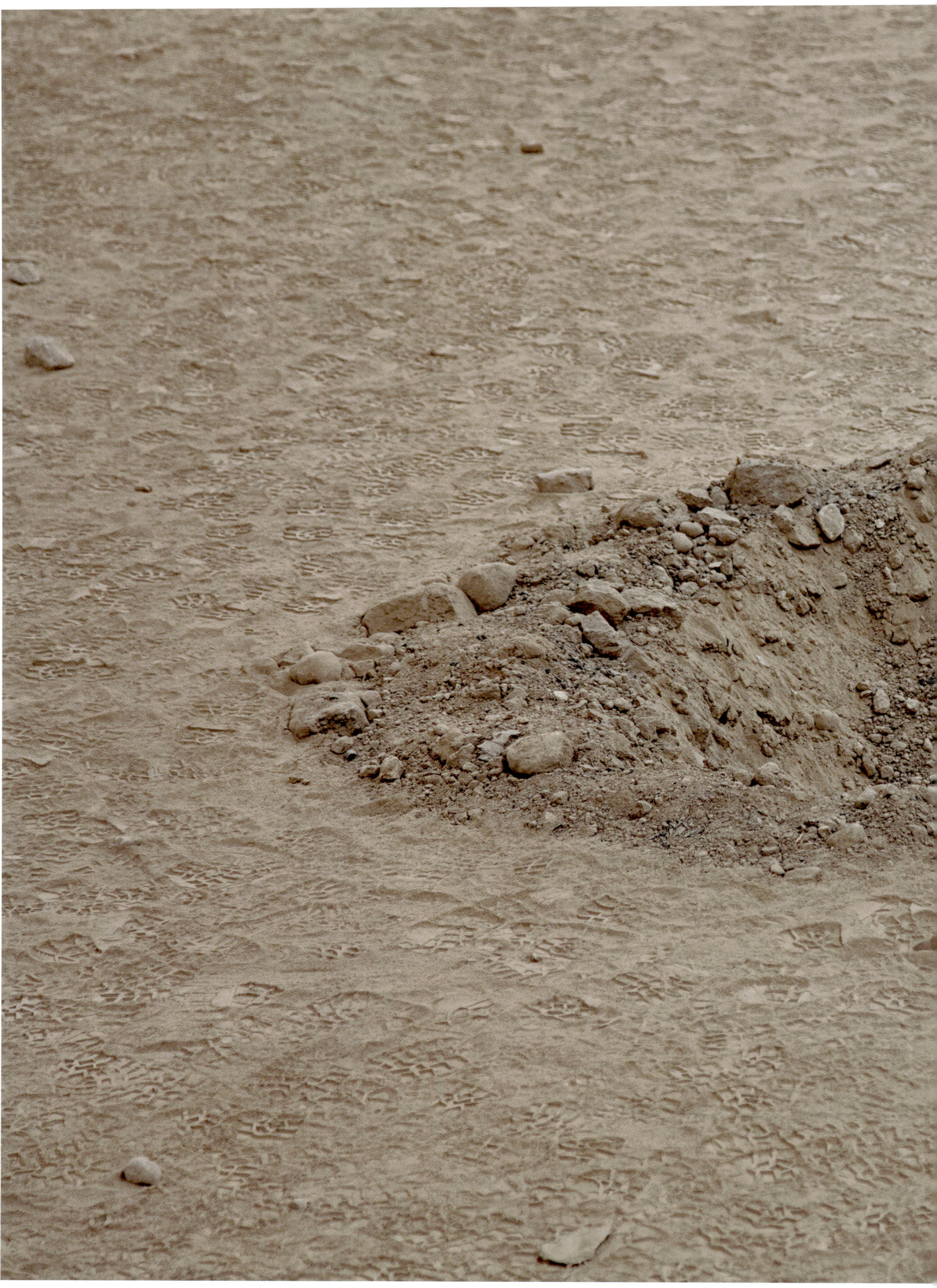

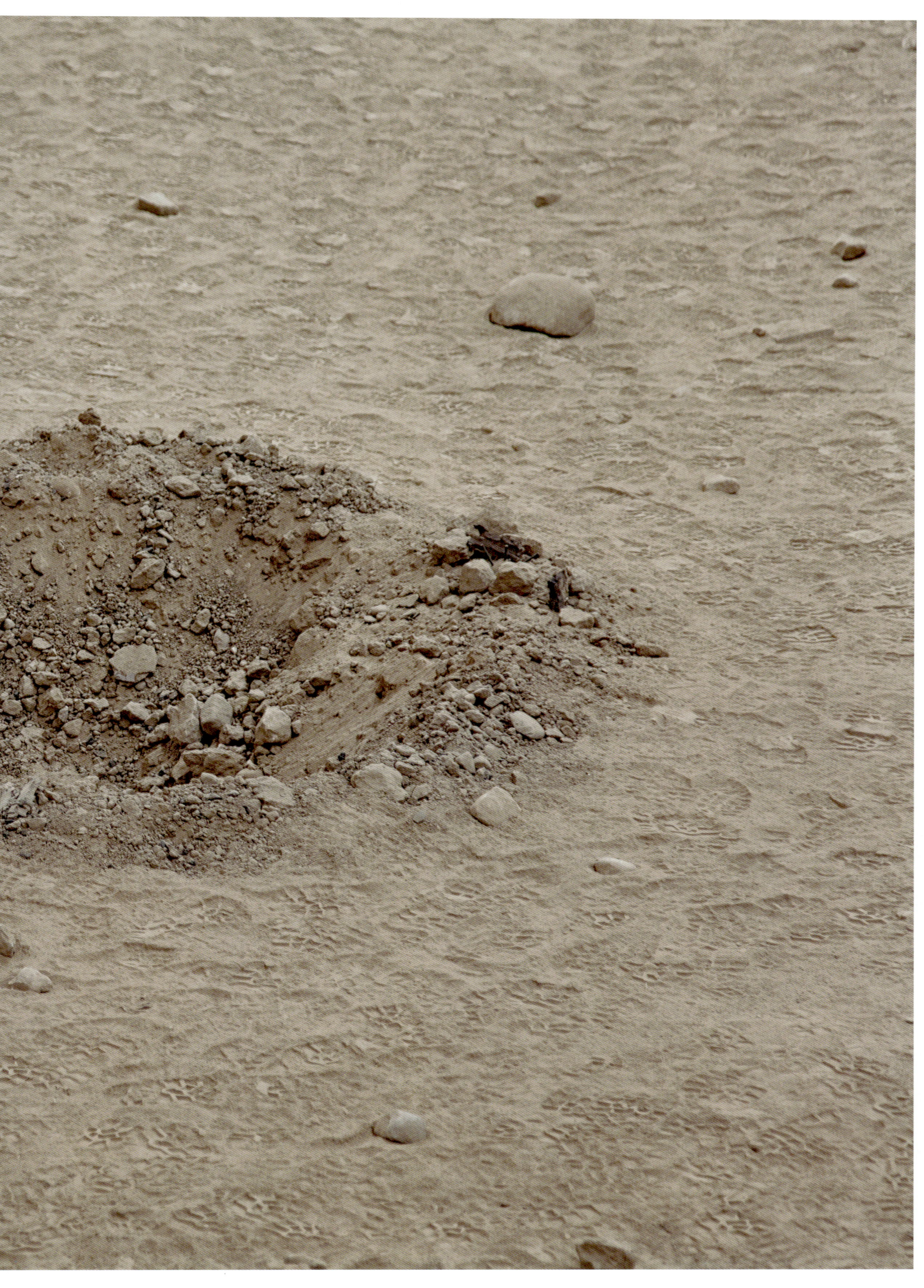

The number of soldiers stationed in the camp has been   [158]
reduced by nearly 90 percent in comparison to when
it was at peak occupancy a few years ago. At that time,
the camp contained some 10,000 people. The outer
perimeter has since remained unchanged, but large
sections of the camp are now uninhabited. At some of
the places where roads intersect are enclosures constructed
from concrete barriers. Inside them, the occasional
pile of scrap metal, discarded junk, trash, or clumps of
weeds. Technically, these areas are also supposed to
be cleared of vegetation regularly and spread with gravel
to prevent the proliferation of gerbils and the sand flies
that accompany them. Those who work in the camp,
however, will tell you again and again: "We can't be
everywhere at once—for that there'd have to be more of
us; everyone's already doing the work of two people here."

Any structures no longer needed following the complete   [160]
withdrawal of the troops will either be abandoned or
sold to local business owners, who can then in turn either
dismantle them or make further use of them right where
they stand once the camp has been closed. The biggest
problem for every construction project and building in
the camp, however, is the soil underneath it. Namely,
a carbonaceous silt mixture that is particularly vulnerable
to underground water erosion, a phenomenon which
has already led in many places in the camp to the lopsided
settling of troop housing and other buildings. To stand
in these lopsidedly sunken structures feels like being on
a ship far from shore on a restless, uneasy sea.

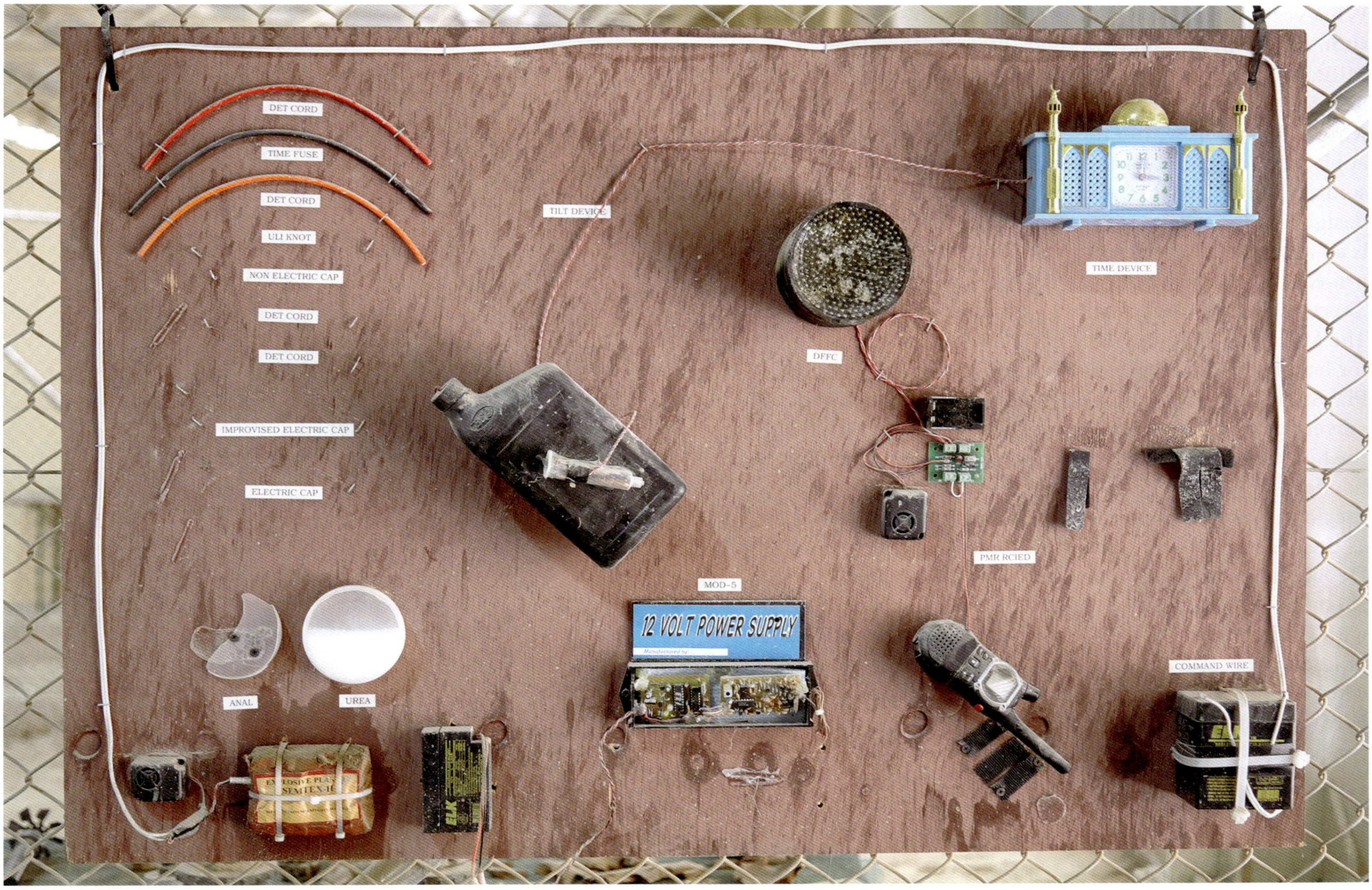

DET CORD
TIME FUSE
DET CORD
ULI KNOT
NON ELECTRIC CAP
DET CORD
DET CORD
IMPROVISED ELECTRIC CAP
ELECTRIC CAP
TILT DEVICE
DFFC
TIME DEVICE
PMR RCIED
ANAL
UREA
MOD-5
12 VOLT POWER SUPPLY
Manufactured by:
COMMAND WIRE
EXPLOSIVE PLAST SEMTEX

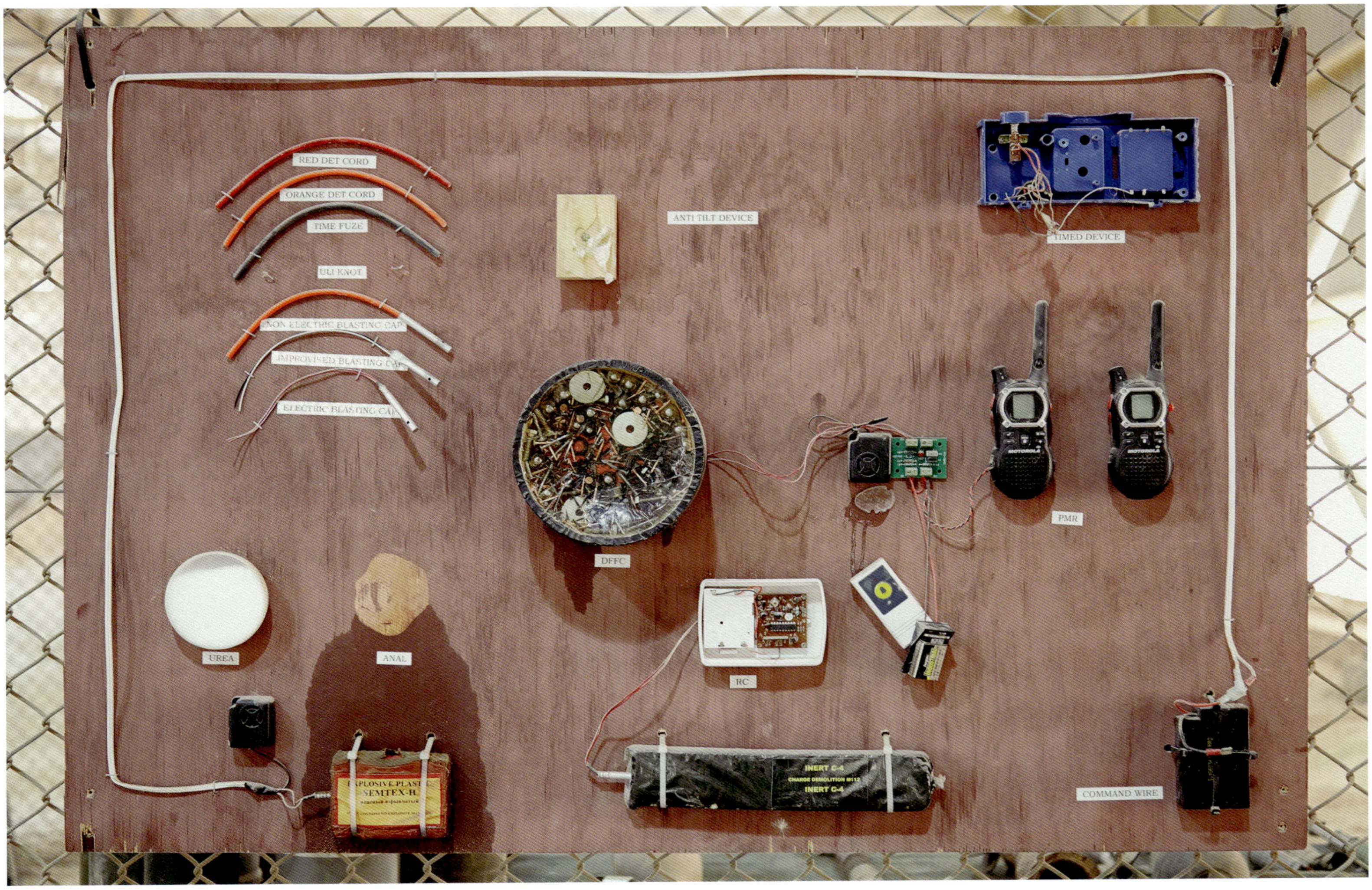

RED DET CORD
ORANGE DET CORD
TIME FUZE
ULI KNOT
NON ELECTRIC BLASTING CAP
IMPROVISED BLASTING CAP
ELECTRIC BLASTING CAP
ANTI TILT DEVICE
TIMED DEVICE
DFFC
PMR
UREA
ANAL
RC
EXPLOSIVE PLAST SEMTEX-H
INERT C-4
CHARGE DEMOLITION M112
INERT C-4
COMMAND WIRE

Whoever is not working at the moment will sometimes sit in a chair in the sun with their shirt off. The German Military has on hand a supply of a sun-blocking lotion manufactured expressly for its desert operations, which all persons within the camp are encouraged to apply frequently. When there's nothing for them to do, soldiers receive what is referred to as *Zeit ZBV*, or "time designated for special use," which more often than not is an abbreviated euphemism for tinkering with various projects, waiting around, playing foosball, and smoking. There is also the opportunity to work out and play sports. The Morale & Welfare Office has a few books available for lending and a small video library, as well as PlayStation consoles and a selection of the most popular current games. Drinking beer is permitted only between the hours of eight and ten pm, and there's a two-can rule in effect. The progression of one's time in deployment, the days, hours, minutes and seconds remaining, as well as the additional income accrued through the tax-exempt Deployment Abroad Bonus *(Auslandsverwendungszuschlag, or AVZ)*, can be tracked on one's smartphone with the help of the AVZ-app. For the desktop computer or laptop, there's a similar program called *The Motivator*, whereby an array of women depicted on the screen become progressively more naked as one's deployment time elapses.

Once that first month of settling in and becoming familiar with their surroundings and circumstances has passed, followed by a period of lethargy, many soldiers deployed abroad become seized by a kind of constructive compulsion. As it does everywhere else in the world, creativity in the camp originates mainly in deprivation and boredom. This penchant for creative pursuits is most conspicuous in the multiple little makeshift bars and individualized places of refuge, out back behind the containers, under camouflage nets or in self-built sanctuaries. In addition to handcrafted furniture and barbecues, one finds here various decorative fretwork pieces, paintings, metal sculptures, small animal enclosures, ornamental gardens and fountains.

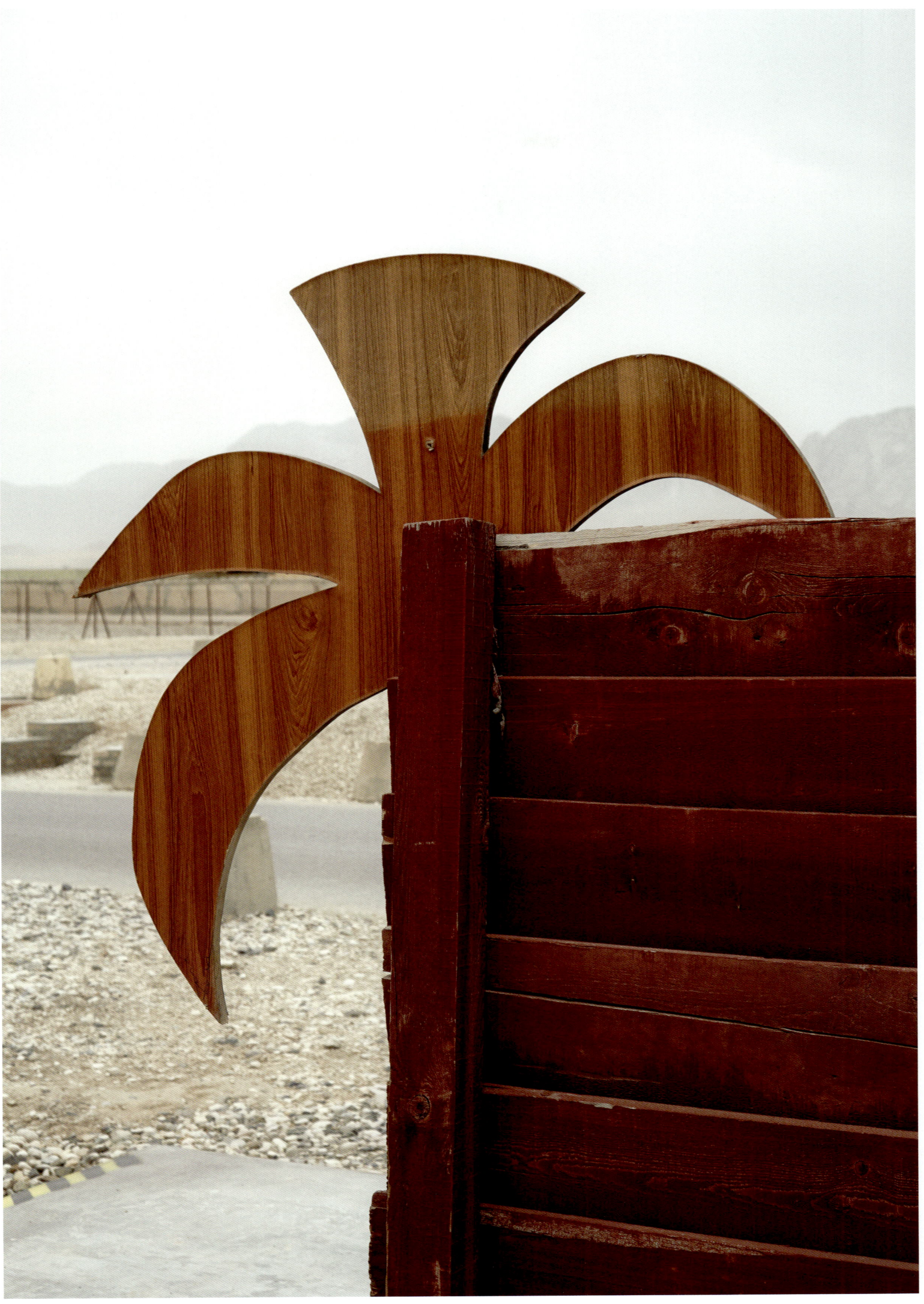

I'm sending the best man I've got—myself.

But you know: He who sits in the lighthouse is always in the dark.

Their shit just rolls right off me anyhow; these days I only answer to love.

And there once again, I'm confronted with my age-old problem: There's only one of me.

Worker protection just ain't worth a jot, 'cause protect us from work it really does not.

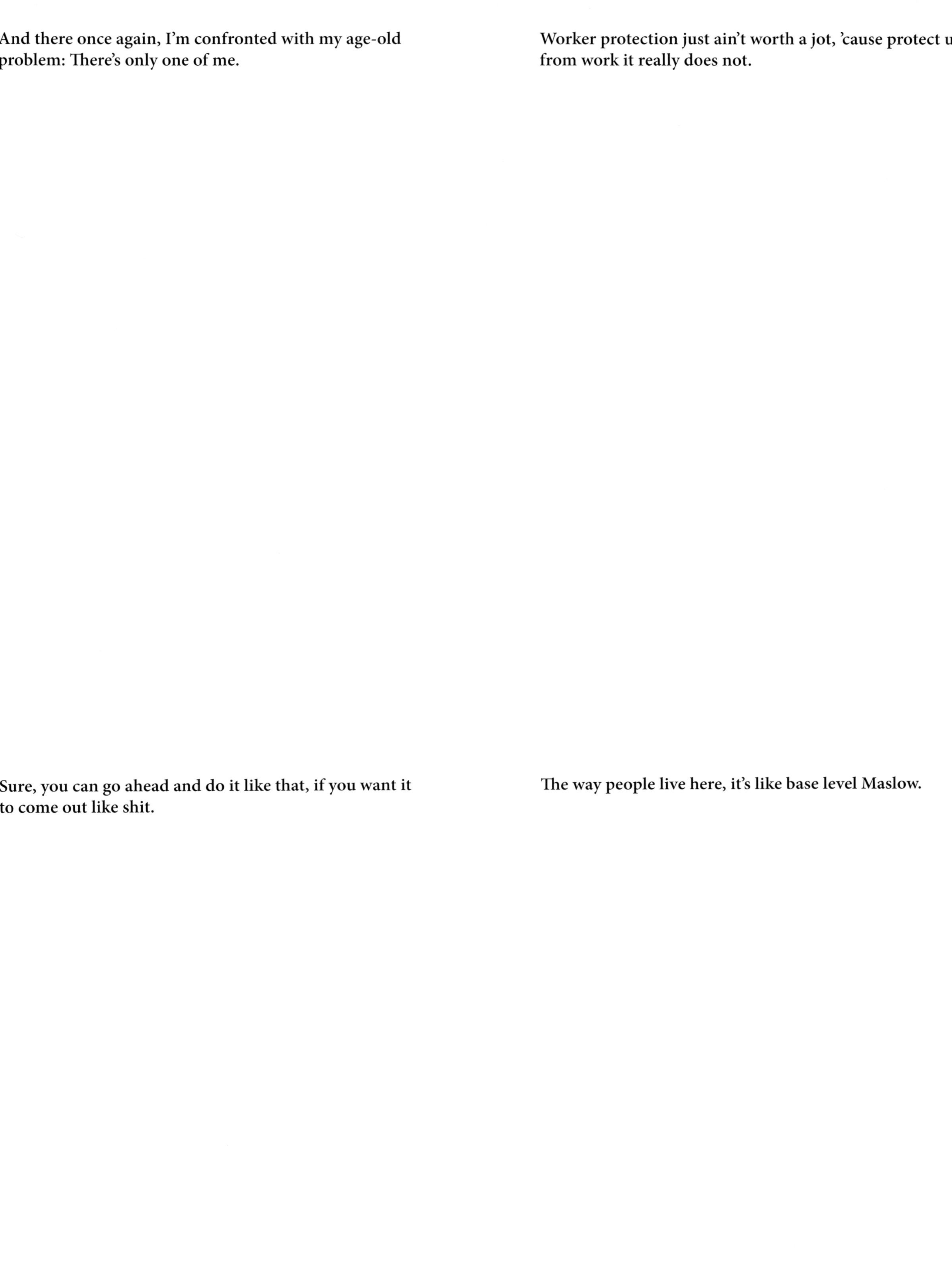

Sure, you can go ahead and do it like that, if you want it to come out like shit.

The way people live here, it's like base level Maslow.

Anyone is redeployable.

We have to be able to appear threatening.

I'm pretty sure I signed something yesterday, though.

Any soldier can submit an application for social events,
and will then be provided with supplies accordingly.

The Afghan is generally known for being very gifted with his hands.

If people are going to die here, it had better be for a good reason.

Connections are only bad for those who don't have any.

We live in a world not yet redeemed.

For these projects the probability of failure is considered greater than zero.

The ground here is unpredictable.

You have to distinguish between those who meet needs and those who have them.

Being a dentist here is also very exciting; the inside of every mouth is like a grab bag full of surprises—stuff you're just not used to seeing anymore, coming from Germany.

The weeks stand still while the days just go on by.

In terms of their behavior, there's actually no difference.

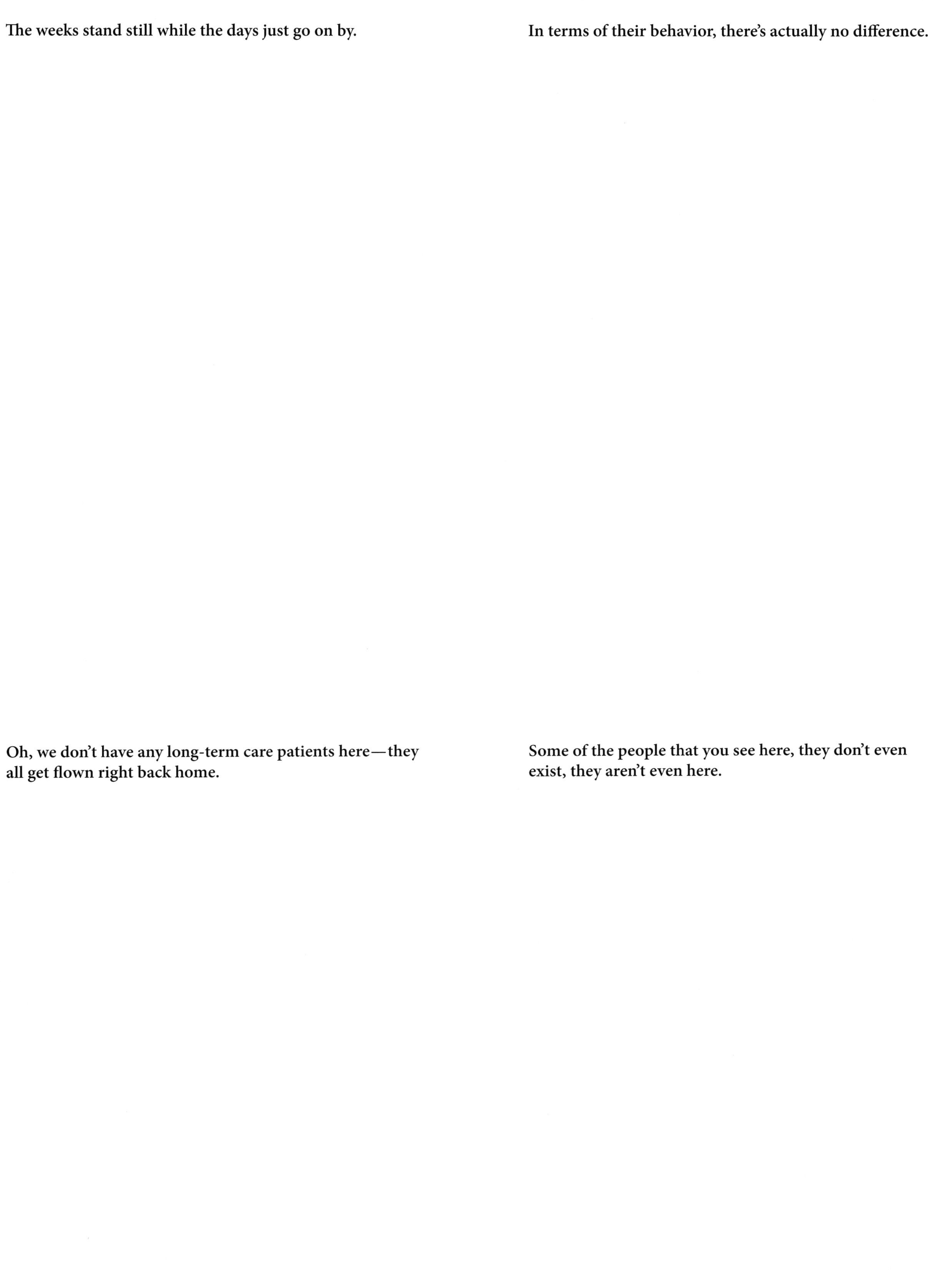

Oh, we don't have any long-term care patients here—they all get flown right back home.

Some of the people that you see here, they don't even exist, they aren't even here.

The enemy isn't supposed to know where we're planning
to reach out to the community; otherwise that's exactly
where they'll go and make for bad headlines.

Any one of us could go out there and fight. The guys who
just fight, that's all they can do.

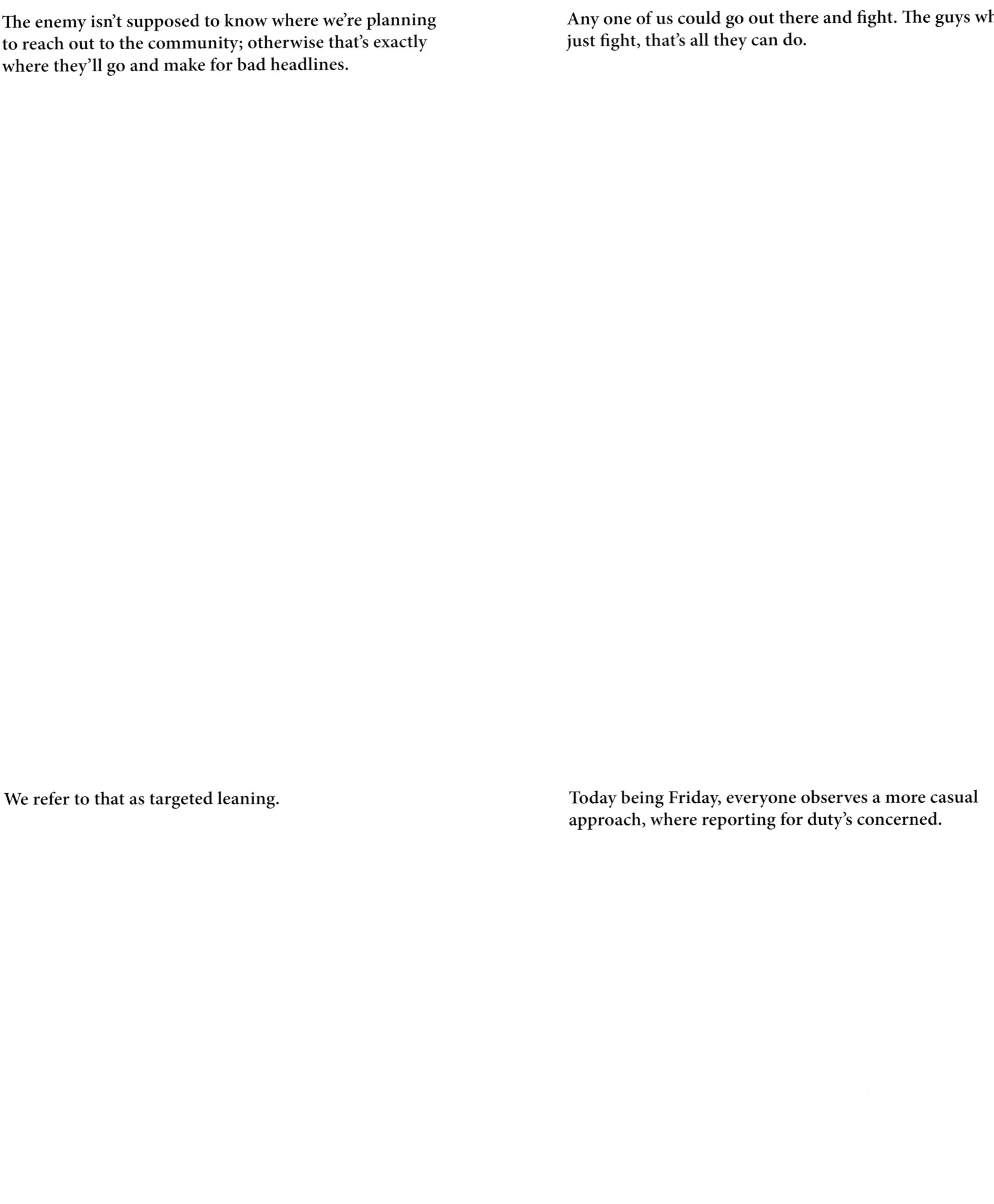

We refer to that as targeted leaning.

Today being Friday, everyone observes a more casual
approach, where reporting for duty's concerned.

One shouldn't get onboard at too high a level; in the end, you're still going to need room for things to escalate.

The Mongols are fierce bastards.

We operate according to the 'beware of dog' principle.

I can't just leave human beings out there just because they're Afghans.

You got to get a fire going in the old stove, if you want to
stay warm.

You know they give people a Big Chicken Dinner for that.

We tend to take the new guys under our wing.

We're the ones with the big stick, and we know how to
use it, too.

If you start talking with an Afghan about politics, then right away you've lost.

Is that something hanging from your jacket, General, sir?

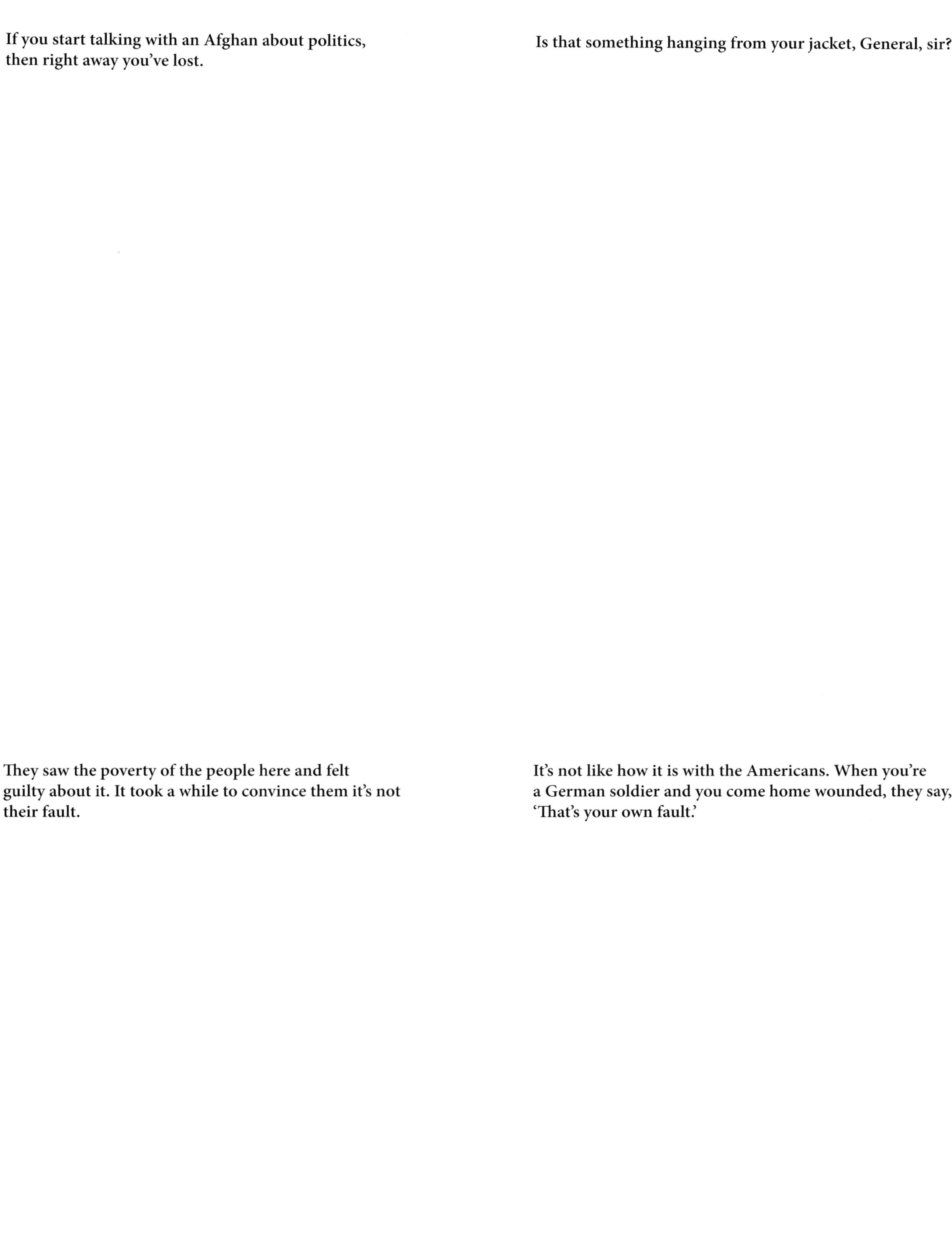

They saw the poverty of the people here and felt guilty about it. It took a while to convince them it's not their fault.

It's not like how it is with the Americans. When you're a German soldier and you come home wounded, they say, 'That's your own fault.'

None of this here has a damn thing to do with
Afghanistan.

Well, I'd say that's pretty ambitious—not to mention
foolish.

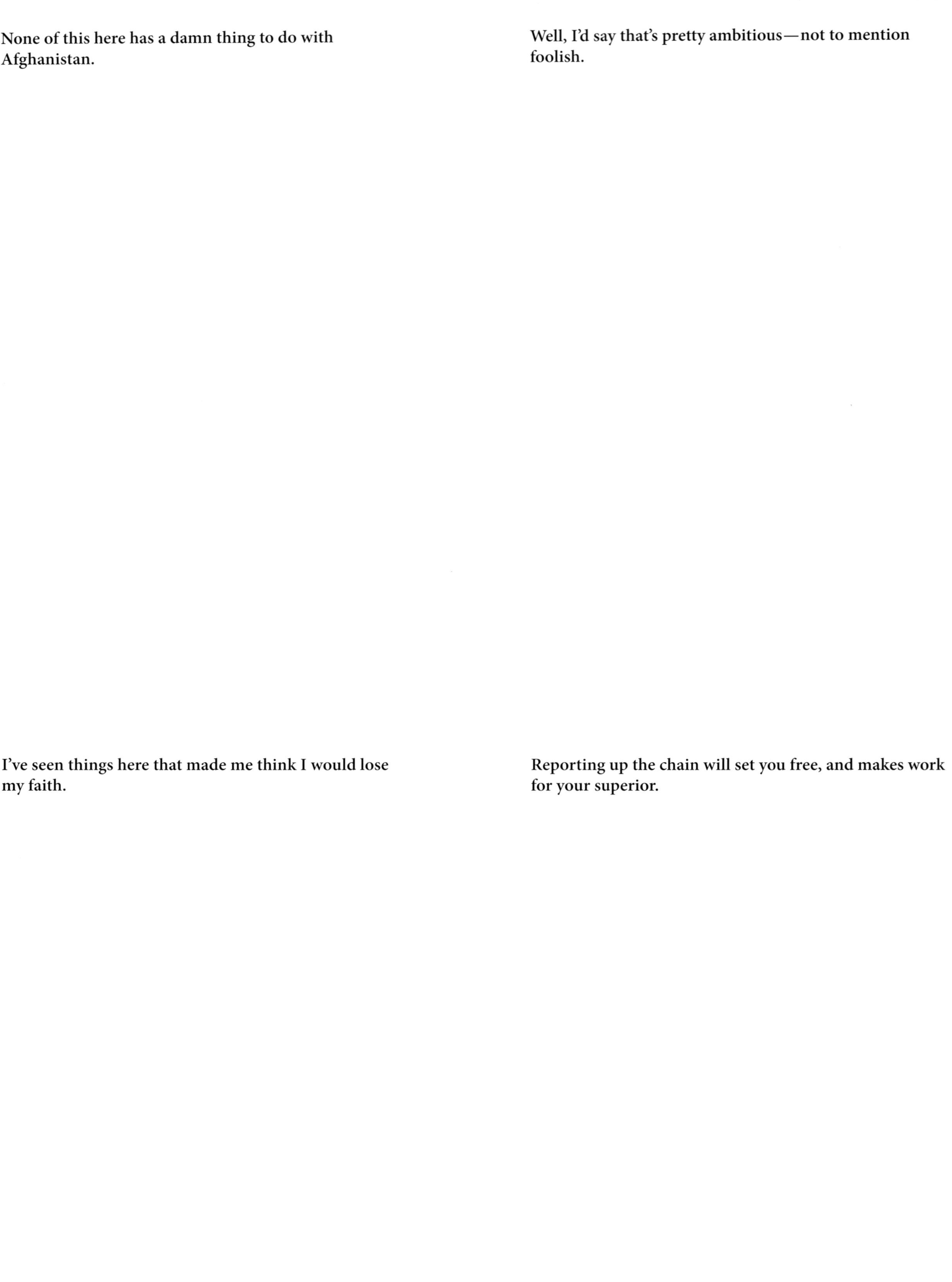

I've seen things here that made me think I would lose
my faith.

Reporting up the chain will set you free, and makes work
for your superior.

A soldier never goes to the can without having a
contingency plan.

[218]

[219]

[220]

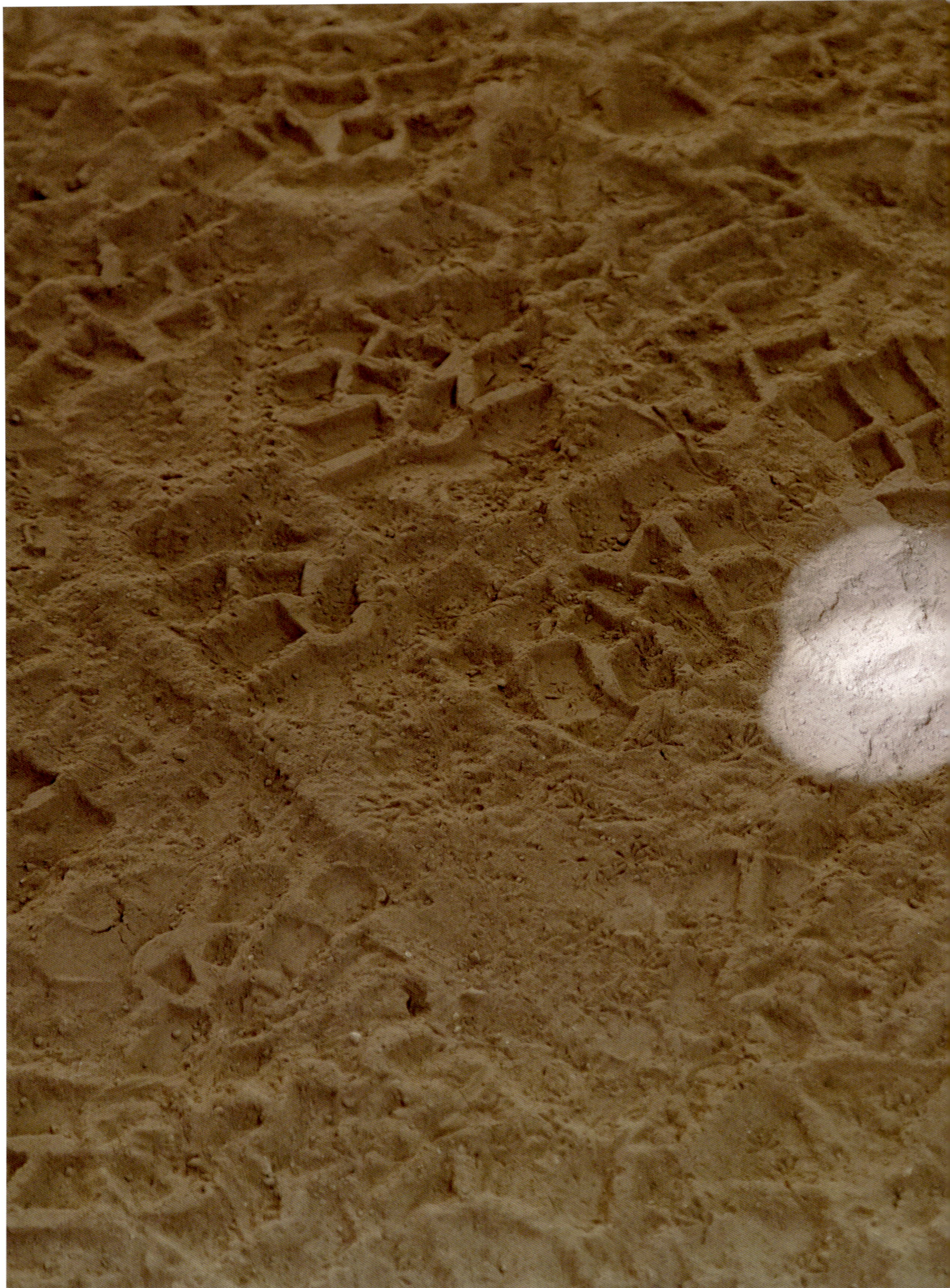

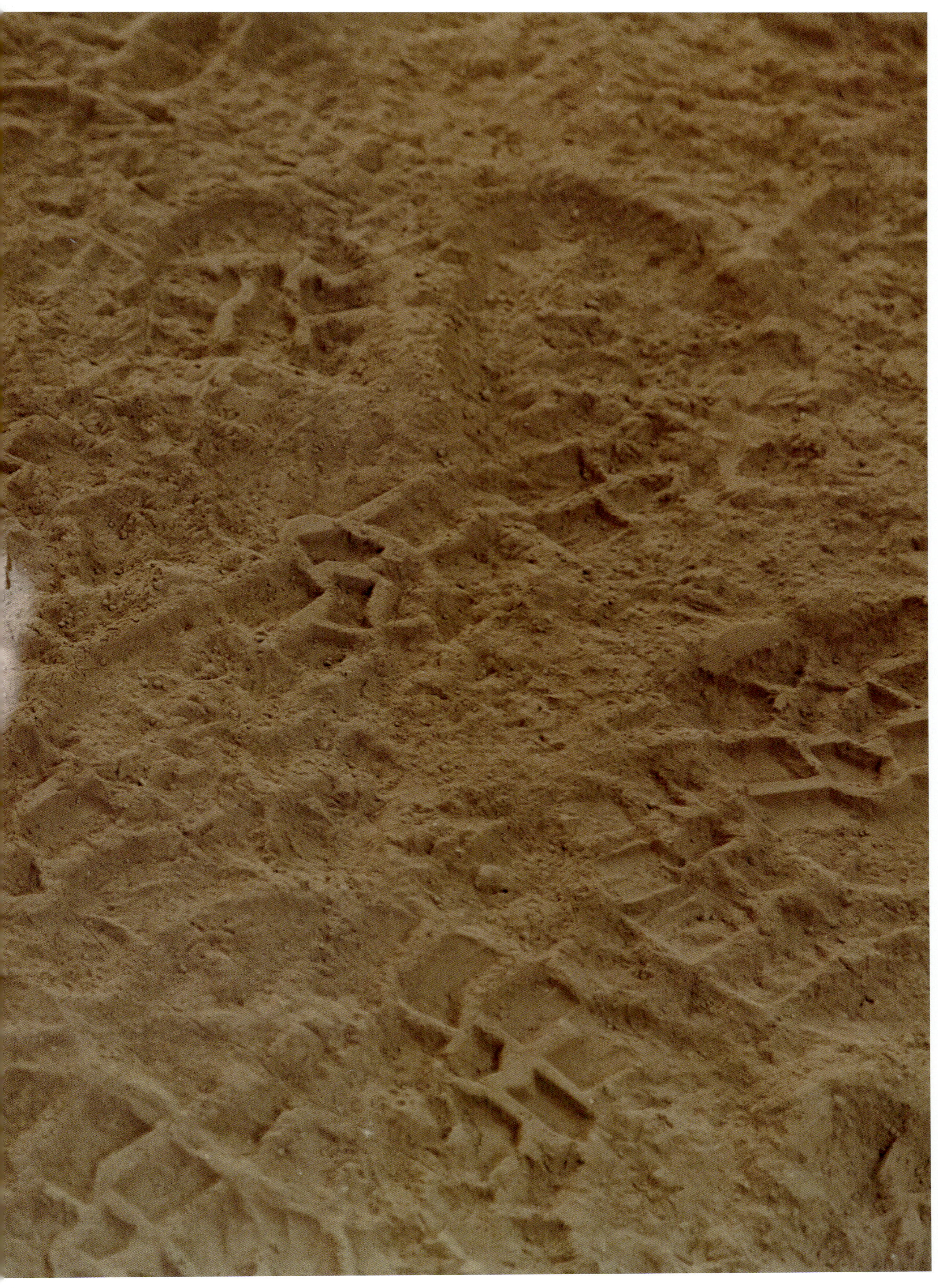

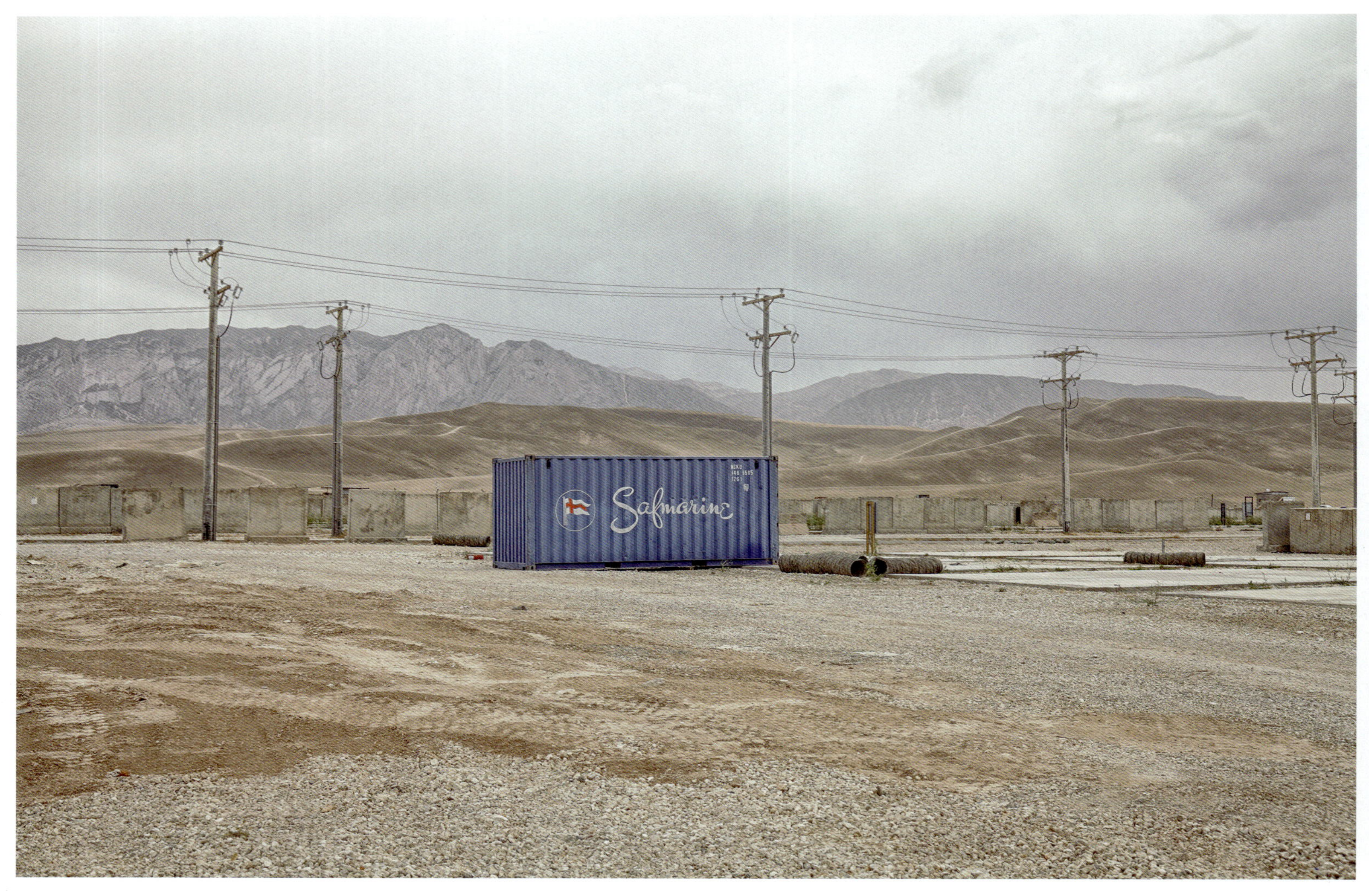

When being shelled, the shutters in the soldiers'
quarters are to be rolled down. It is also recommended to
relocate to the corridor.

[232]

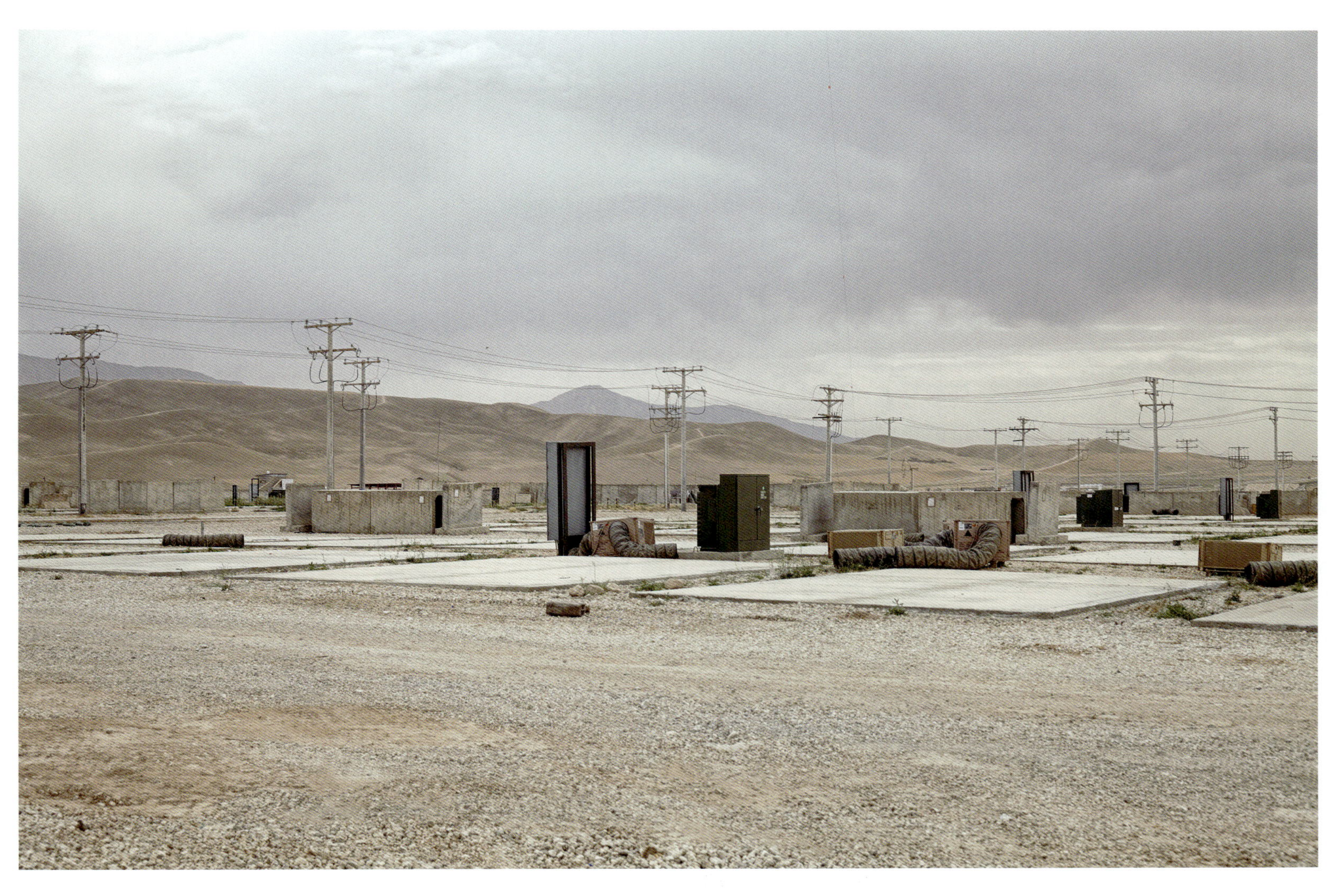

[235]   [236]

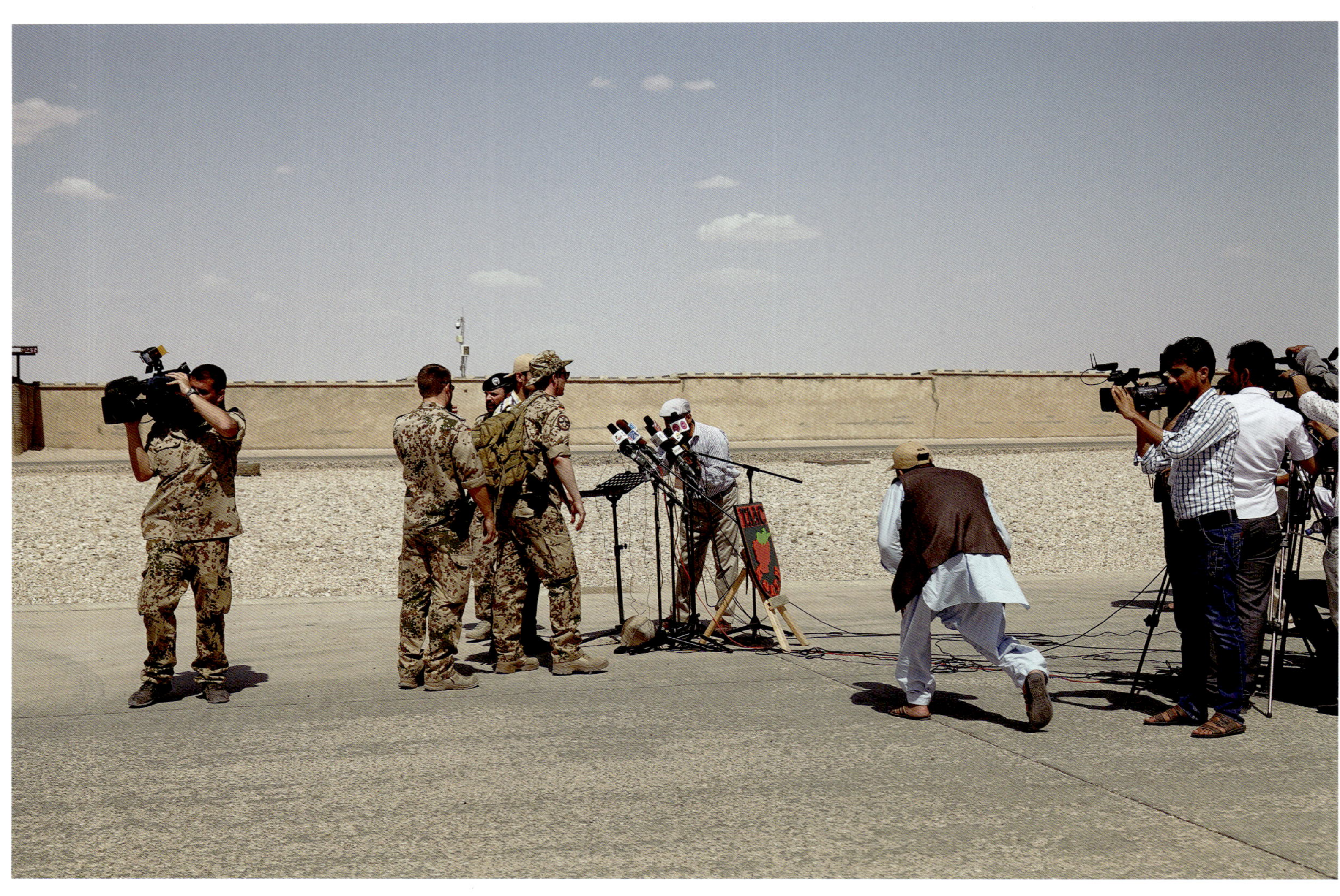

[239]

Overseen by the Center for Operative Communications (formerly Psychological Warfare), "Radio Andernach" is the German military's own broadcasting station, featuring among others the program *Good Morning Afghanistan*, which can only be listened to in areas of operation on VHF radio or via the internet following a successful login by members of the German Armed Forces and their families. It's possible to call in with greetings and song dedications from the homeland. The most frequently requested songs at the station last year were Helene Fischer's "Atemlos durch die Nacht," "Happy" by Pharrell Williams, and Linkin Park's "One Step Closer." The real hit song of the summer for the camp's German contingent, however, and the one receiving accordingly the most airplay, was "Unter meiner Haut" by Gestört aber Geil. Despite them being on average too young to fit the profile for its target audience, there is exhibited among the camp's temporary residents a distinct soft spot for traditional German folk music. It's suspected, however, that once they've returned home to Germany, this affinity will prove short-lived.

[241]

Also located on the premises of the camp's local radio station is a rehearsal space, complete with instruments and amplifiers. Since bands can only form for brief periods within the limits of their members' respective deployments, playing for example at the contingents' going away parties, the material they rehearse and perform consists predominantly of cover versions. Founded by soldiers in the camp, the band *Sprengbrand* has made a recording in the Radio Andernach studio of a song that they composed themselves, titled "The Grey Bird." The song is a ballad which tells the story of the German Air Force plane that delivers the soldiers to the camp and carries them home again.

[243]

[244]

In the Atrium, a courtyard located in the heart of the camp and girded on all four sides by single-story buildings and a shaded arbor, soldiers can be found throughout the day resting on patio furniture arranged in the shadows around the bright sunlit square. A few of them stare drowsily at laptop screens, while others sit together in groups and talk. A stage has been erected in the courtyard for the information event held at the beginning of each deployment and for the closing party thrown at its conclusion.

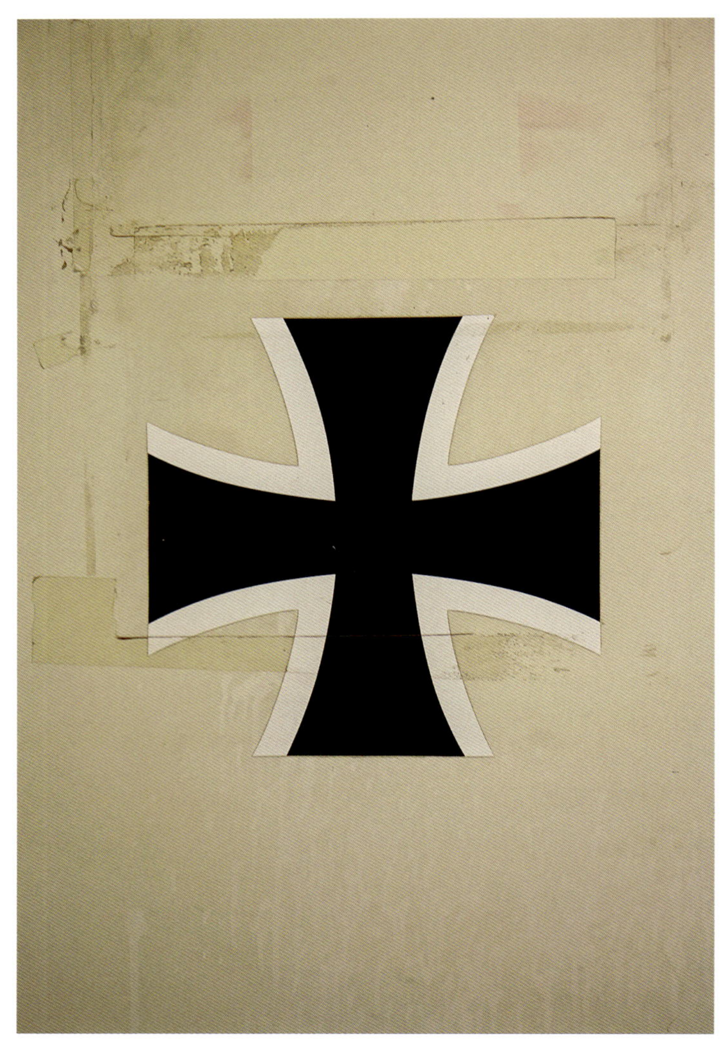

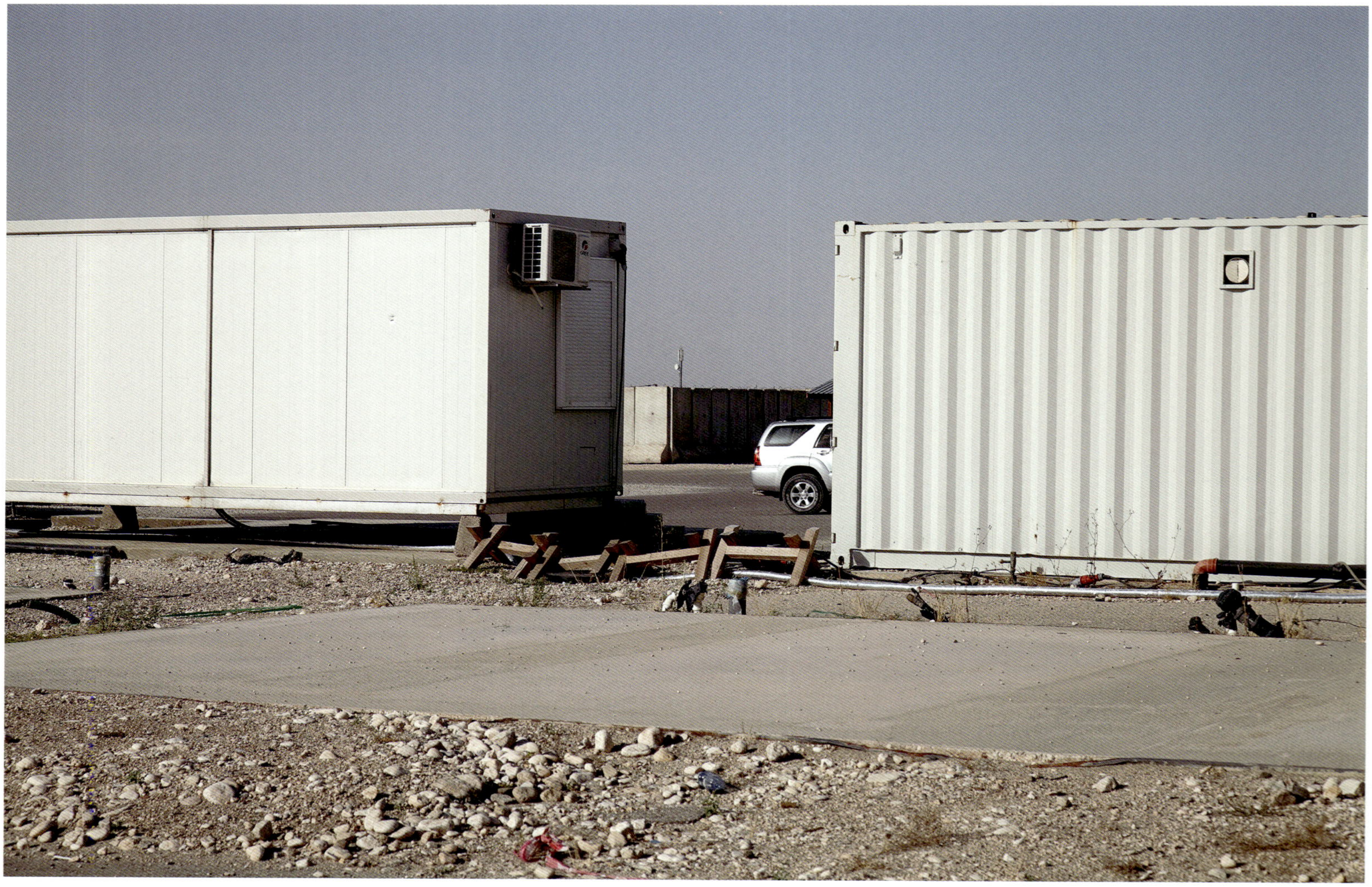

One of the buildings surrounding the courtyard house is the Morale & Welfare Office. Here a friendly support staff officer is entrusted with renting out badminton rackets, darts, board games, DVDs, books, televisions, PlayStations, fog machines, and other technical equipment for events, as well as managing waiting lists and booking schedules for the badminton court and mini-soccer field. His work area consists of an improvised counter in front of which is assembled a frequently changing collection of decorative objects. An old first aid kit, a surfboard, a stuffed flamingo, and plastic flowering vines constitute the seasonal décor for summer. Of course, for Christmas the decorations will be changed accordingly.

When asked, the support staff officer explains that it is very important to him to come into contact and converse with the people here. He says he took on a deployment abroad in order to experience something new. On his own initiative, he has learned a bit of Dari. Over the Easter holidays, he organized a small market where various national dishes were served. There was also an Easter bonfire, summer-skiing, an egg-and-spoon race, life-size live-action foosball, and Highland games. There's a whodunit mystery dinner held regularly in the 'Oase' support facility, not to mention poker tournaments and open air bingo.

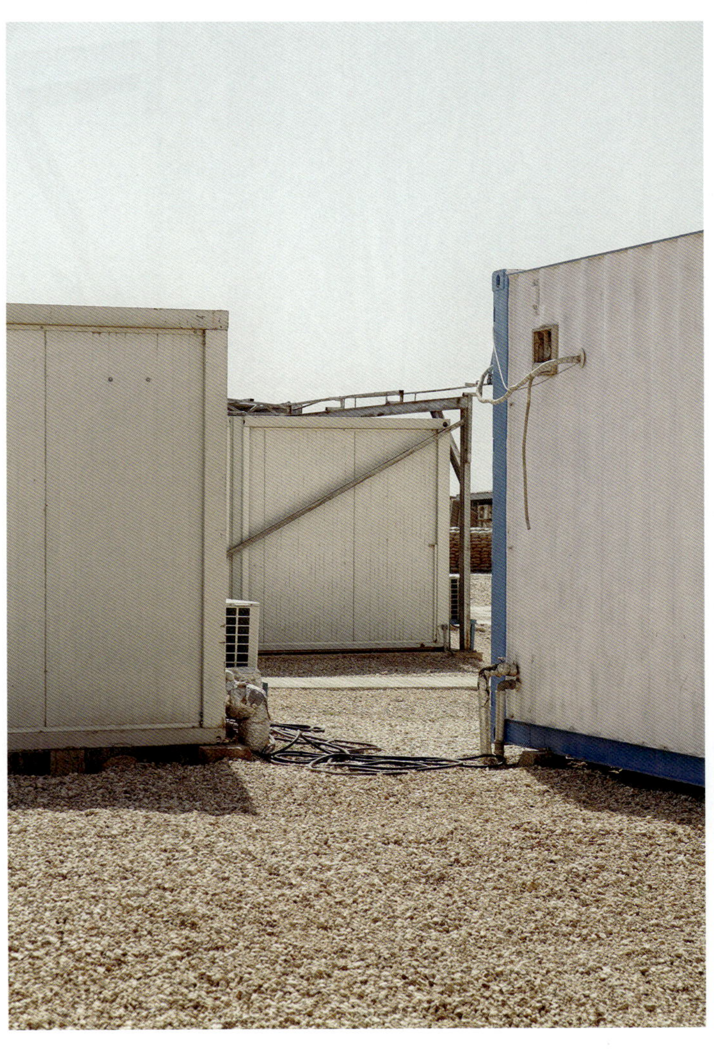

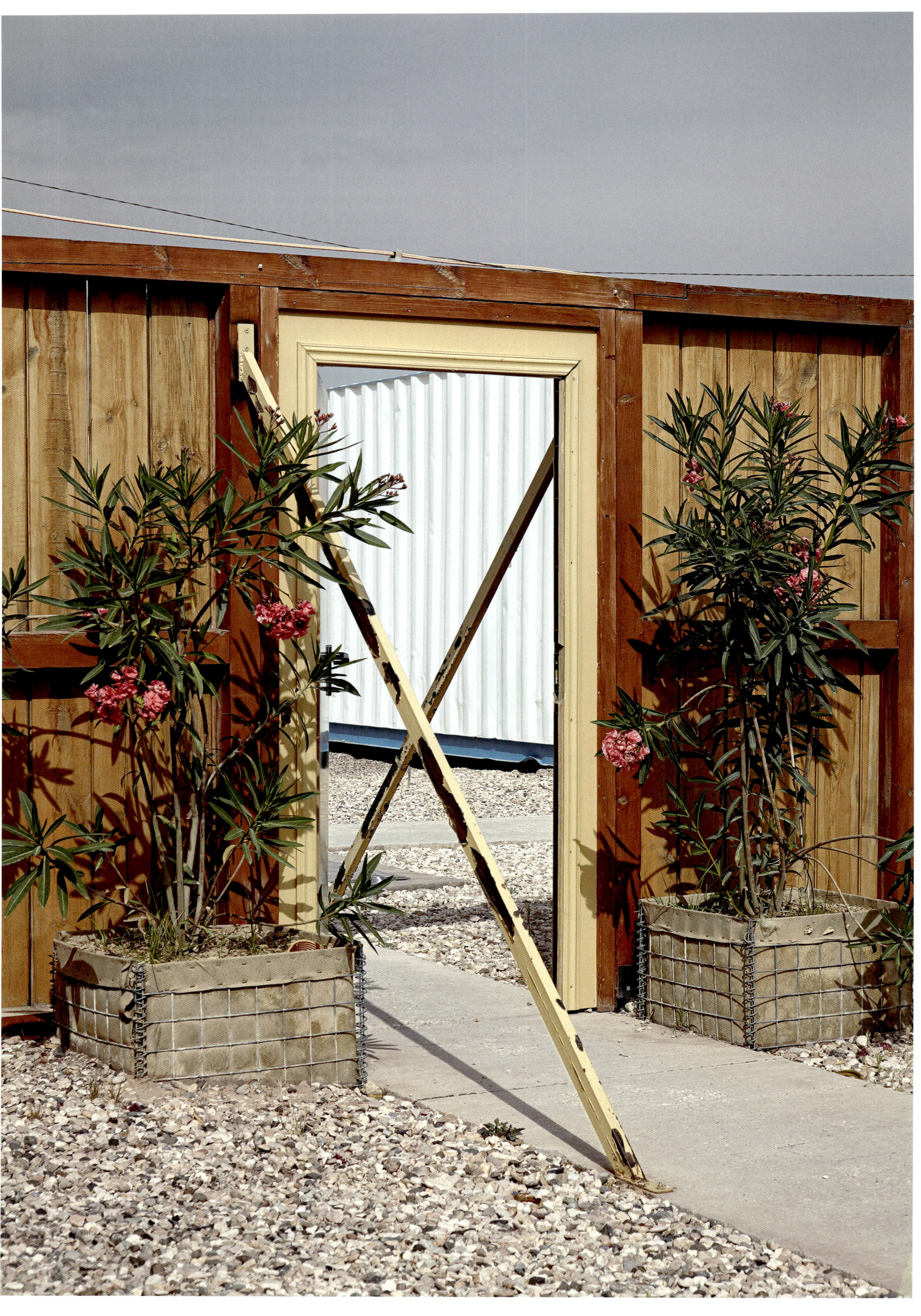

The support staff officer's job also includes organizing charity events for the shelter for orphans and widows in the nearby city. For the orphaned kids, the camp regularly hosts a Children's Day. The support staff officer says he's convinced that, even without weapons, one can help out on the ground here as a soldier.

Among those working with him are eight locals, with whom he's very pleased. The support staff officer admits that of course it can be difficult to expand one's own horizons while in the camp if one isn't actively doing something about it, in other words, engaging socially with others—with the ones who get to occasionally go outside of the camp and return, but also with those who come from elsewhere originally. He acknowledges that in this sense, the experiences can really only be had second-hand, through the stories of others.

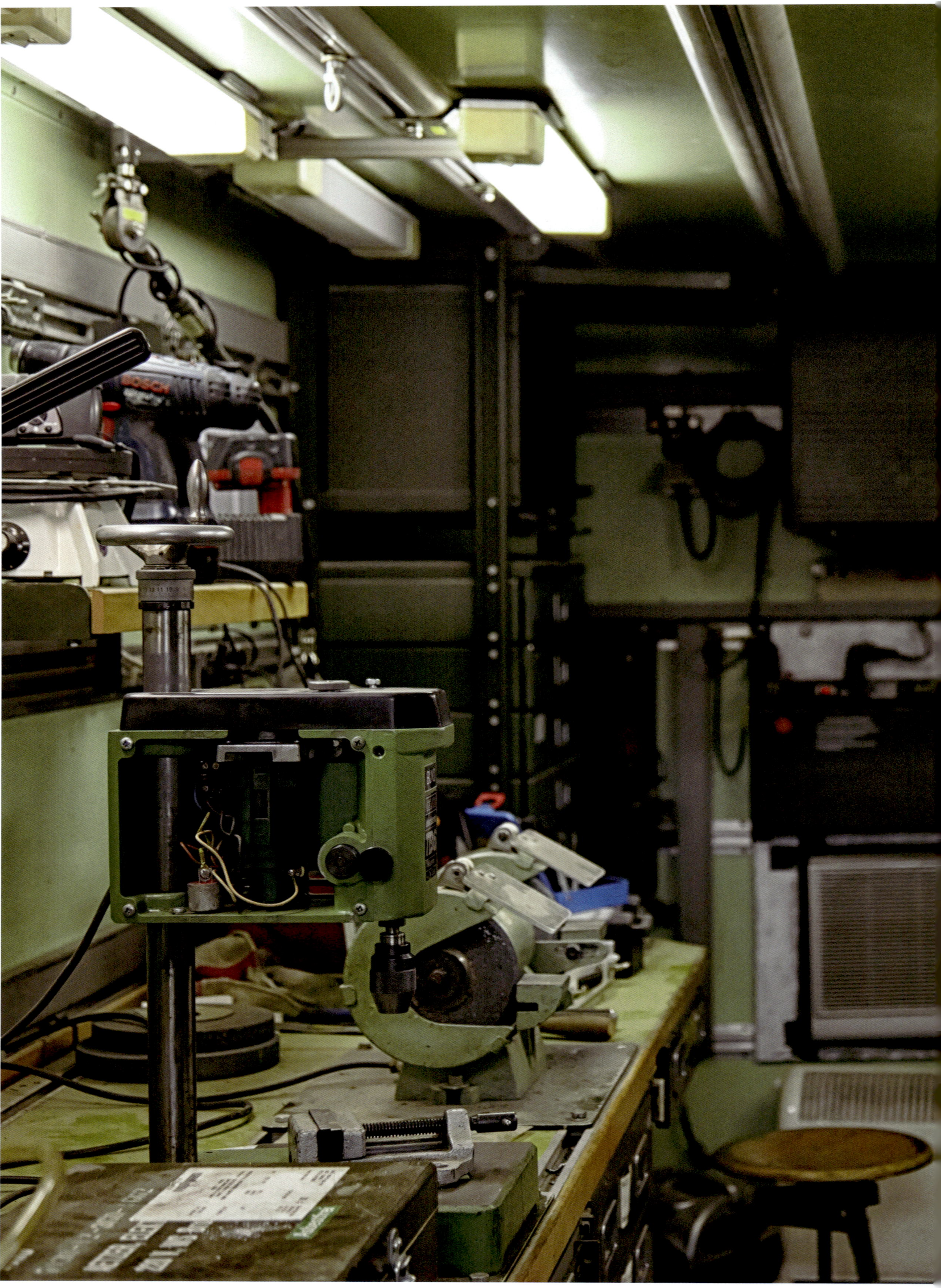

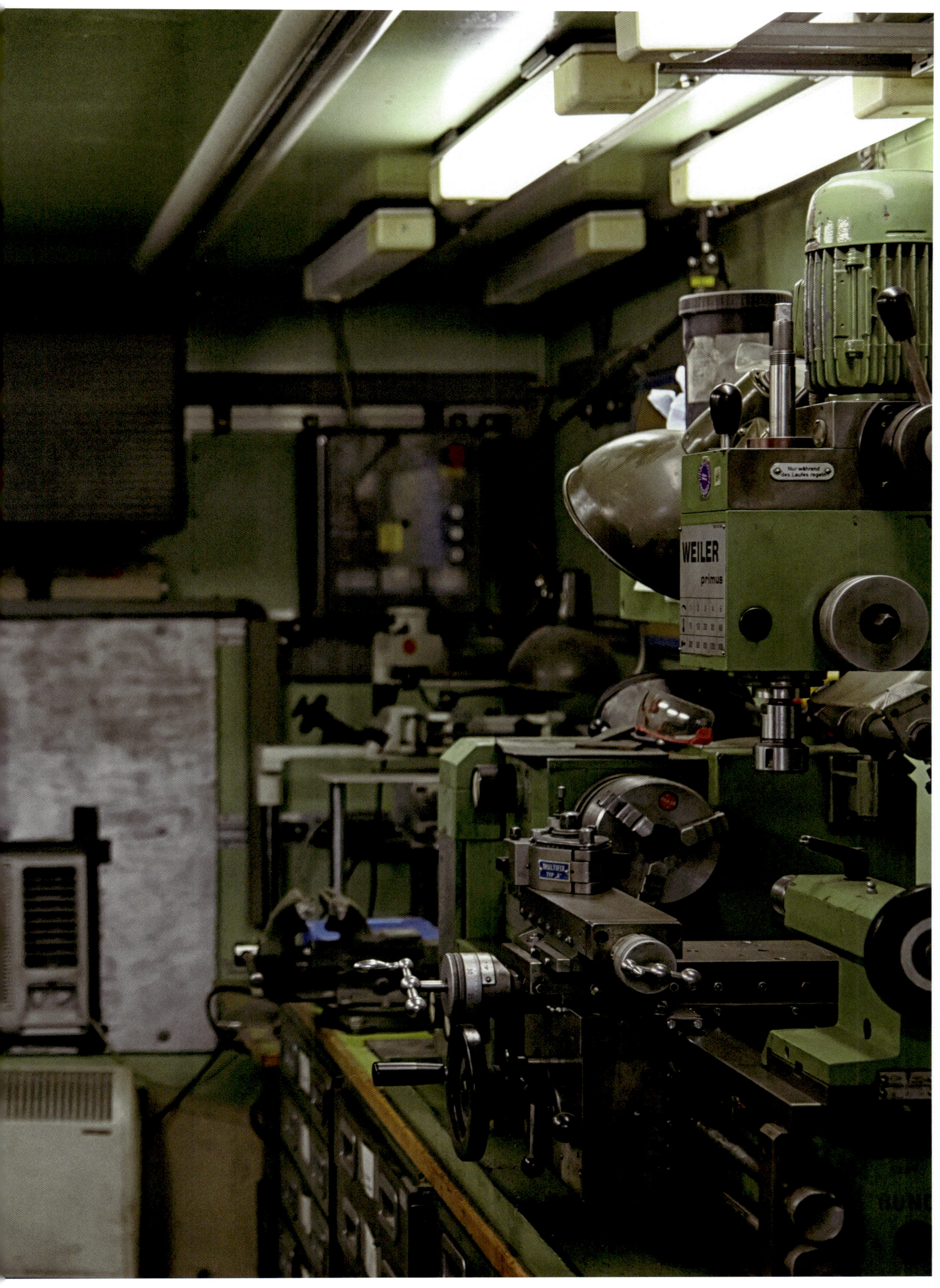

Nur während
des Laufes regeln
WEILER
primus

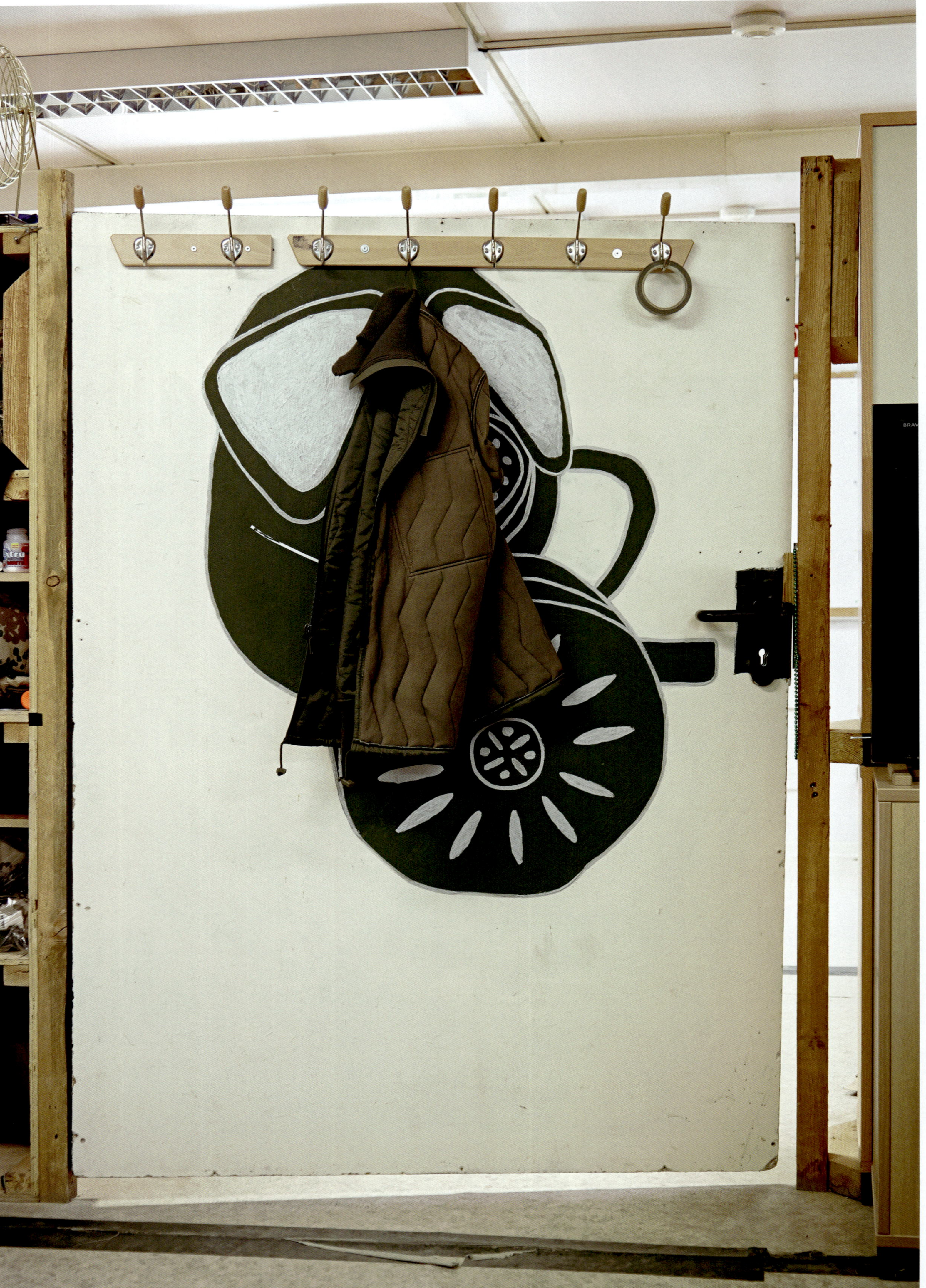

The camp's choir has rehearsal every Tuesday in the camp
church. The military chaplain and a young female soldier
along with six older gentlemen position themselves in
a semicircle and sing to the accompaniment of an acoustic
guitar, electric piano, and trumpet. The altar in the camp
church is a plain grey stone topped with a lectern.
Affixed to the front of an evidently handmade altar candle,
a rather plump Jesus hangs on his cross and gazes out
contentedly into the room.

[274]

[275]

Sitting on top of the container in front of the camp
hospital is a hand-built sailboat, a single-masted, with the
German flag and a mainsail of green hoisted aloft and a
human skeleton in a pirate costume standing at the wheel,
grinning eternally as it stares out over the camp and
its barrier walls, away towards the nearby mountains.
Written on the ship's flank in white lettering is the name
Charon: the ferryman of the mythological underworld
who transports the dead across the river Styx and into the
kingdom of Hades. German naval doctors built this ship
for their contingent's departing fleet doctor to honor
him in his role as captain during their time in the camp.
Subsequent contingents then expanded on this parting
gift, transforming it into the Death Ship and installing the
skeletal ferryman at its helm. Situated beneath the Death
Ship are the lounge area and the small bar that serves
the medical platoon. Camouflage netting obstructs the
direct view the doctors and medics who drink and talk
here in the evenings would otherwise have of the ferryman
Charon.

How on previous tours of duty, he'd been deployed as a close protection officer, and so was hardly ever in the camp, staying instead overnight in crude outposts, in the mud, in tiny tents, with nights spent on guard duty with no sleep, always in danger and always under stress, how at some point he'd thought to himself, "Ok, now you've had your fun, now it's time to grow up," recalls the first sergeant in the container housing the psychological counseling center—how he'd subsequently participated in an advanced training program and now, as a troop psychological counselor, assists the lead psychologist with her work in the camp. Thanks to his experience, he says his fellow soldiers regard him as a peer, and this immediately earns him their trust. Of course it also doesn't hurt that on his previous deployments he was one of the ones who was exposed to danger out there, that he knows what that feels like. The troop psychologist interjects that, on that first tour of duty, everybody's personal norm shatters under the pressure of the concrete threat and fear of dying. A feeling of solidarity emerges, a camaraderie, a sort of boy scout romanticism—you think that on your first deployment abroad you've made at least twenty new friends for life, and out of those you stay in touch with maybe one of them, but that doesn't matter.

Only a few find the experience of living here together for months in close quarters to be a burden. At any rate, it's not one of the problems brought regularly to the attention of the troop psychological counseling team. It's much more often the case that the soldiers manage to create even closer spaces, personal places of refuge, small enclaves, says the first sergeant—that they form little groups within the larger mass of uniformed men and women. These badges that they wear on their sleeves are also significant here, he says. He's referring to the embroidered cloth patches about the size of beer coasters, for which blank areas ready with Velcro are provided on the uniforms so that the soldiers can affix their own individual emblems there. In a corner of the camp near the main gate, there exists a small market at which local merchants sell lapis lazuli, rugs, and tea things, but also these sleeve patches, embroidered with different motifs if desired.
The first sergeant is convinced that, following their return to their home country, the soldiers are, at least for a while, better people. For the approximately four to six months that it takes for them to adjust and become reacclimated, they're more sensitive than usual, and examine more closely and critically their consumerism and how they take the circumstances of their lives for granted.

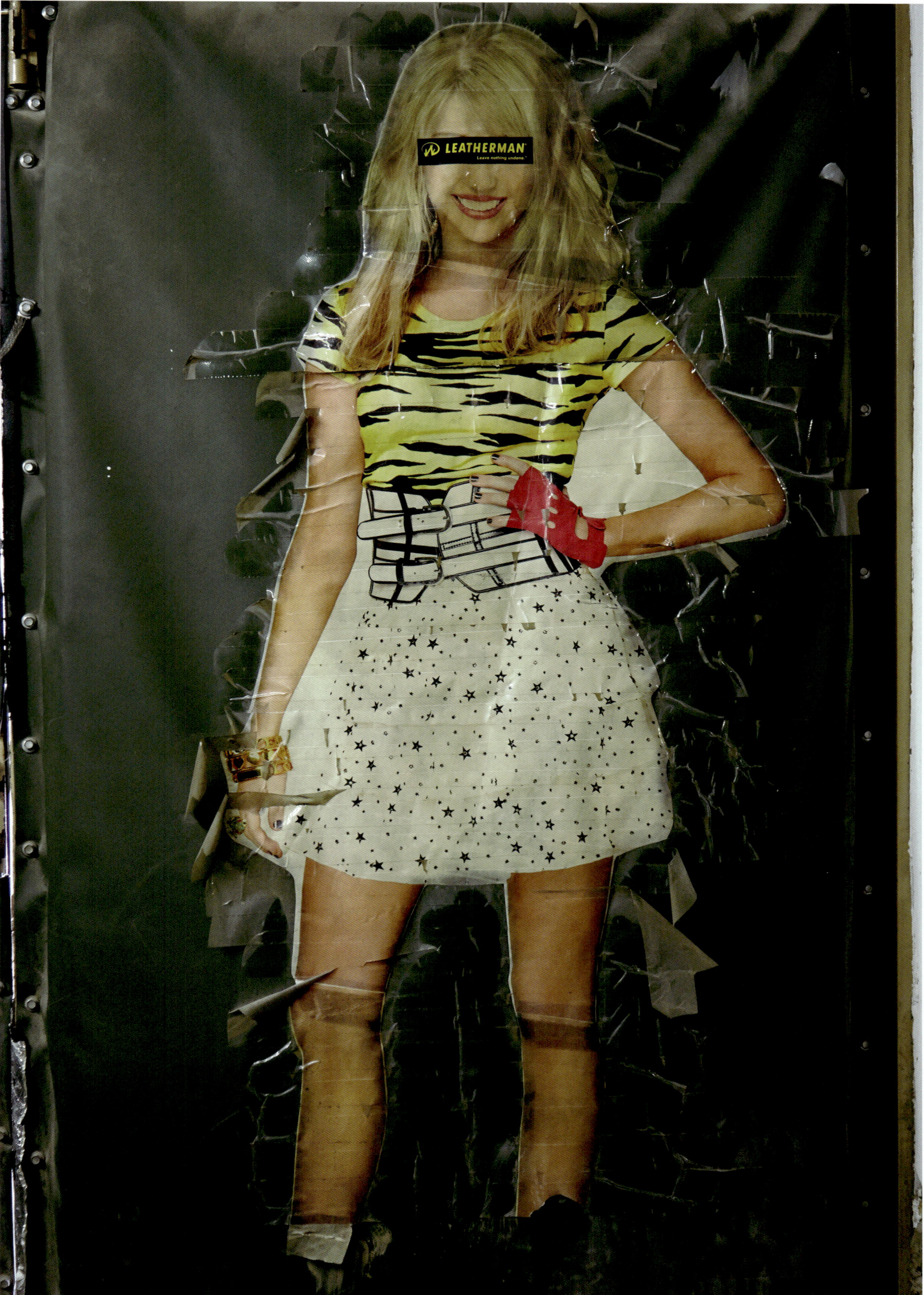

LEATHERMAN
Leave nothing undone.™

The frequent use of metaphors around playing, scouting,
and summer camp could give the outward impression
that the military is also a place where you don't have to grow
up if you don't want to.

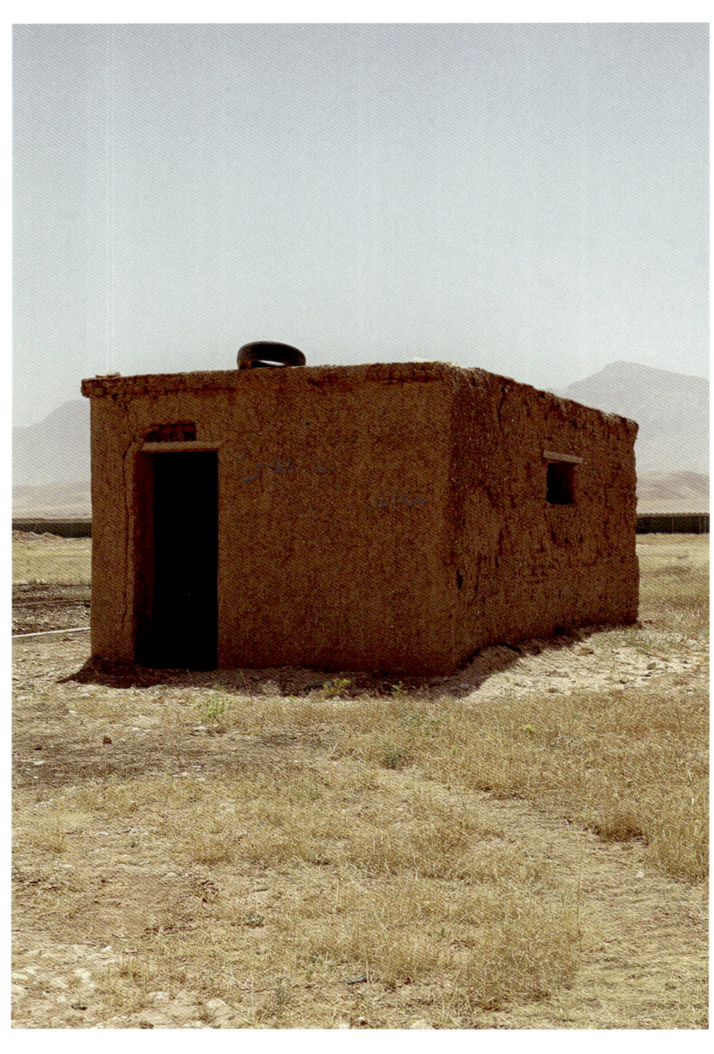

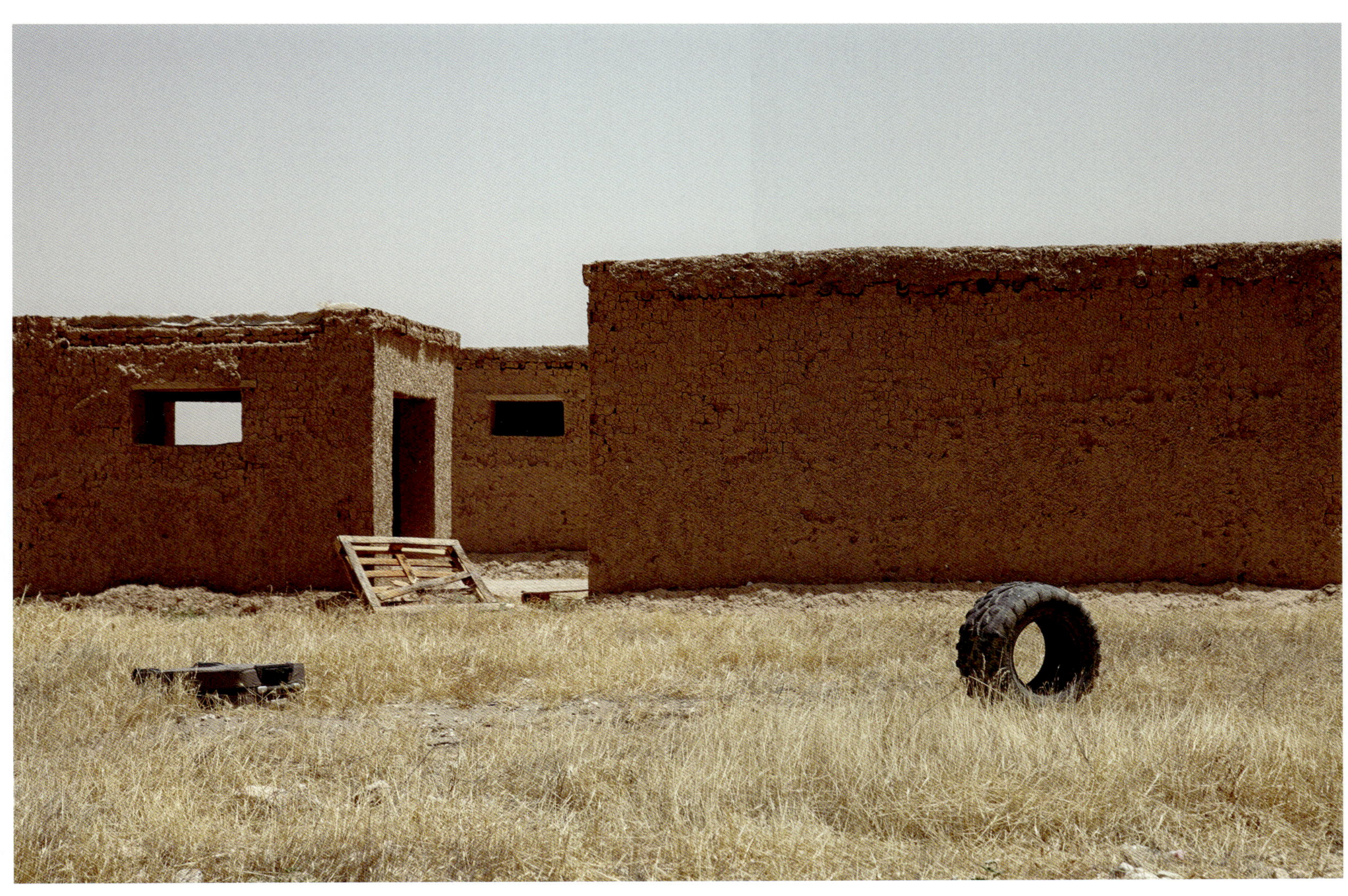

[291]

In the days when soldiers would more frequently go on missions outside of the camp, they could be divided into four different groups:

the ones who were happy they didn't have to go
the ones who would have been happy to go
the ones who went and were happy about it
the ones who had to go and were not happy about it

These days, this is rarely still an issue by the time they get to the camp. Now they can decide already at home to which group they would like to belong.

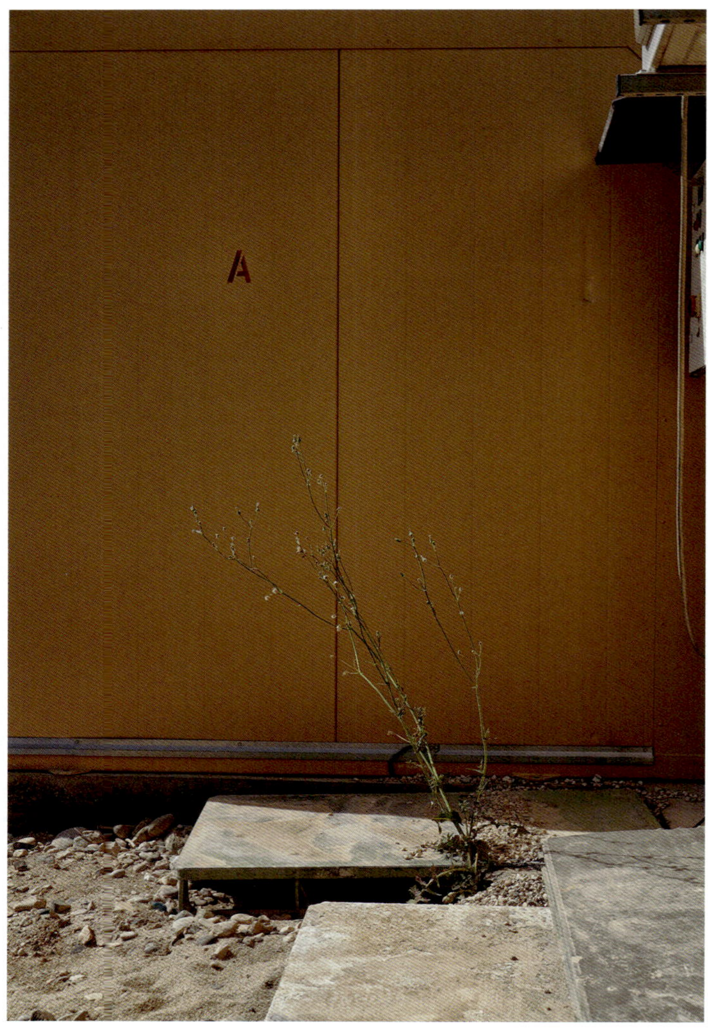

A stretch of the camp's airfield patched with fresh cement and a red *R* mark the impact site of a short-range missile that was fired at the camp from the mountains with an improvised rocket launcher.

Usually missiles launched from these types of improvised artillery land somewhere in the surrounding country-side, as they can't really be aimed as much as just pointed roughly in the general direction of the camp, and those firing them are in all likelihood waiting for the launch behind a rock with their hands over their ears. This one missile, however, managed to detonate inside the camp. No one was injured, although slivers of metal were found in buildings and vehicles within a wide radius of the blast site. Fortunately, nobody had been working in the immediate vicinity.

Those who were already serving in the camp at the time speak of the explosion as having had the effect of a wake-up call among the soldiers. The complacency into which they'd been lulled by the semblance of relative safety inside the camp was replaced for a time with a renewed alertness, a state of high alarm, of diligent watching and listening. It soon became clear to most, however, that even this heightened vigilance would have no effect on their own immanent security situation. They would have to put their trust in those guarding the camp.

The so-called fundamental right to conscientious objection also applies to soldiers on active duty. Since the suspension of compulsory military service in June of 2011, approximately 1,400 in-service members of the German Armed Forces have made use of this right. The application for conscientious objector status is to be submitted to the German Armed Forces Career Center, and the person applying subsequently transferred to non-combatant service. These days, soldiers who become conscientious objectors are no longer bullied, berated, and verbally abused by their superiors, or denounced in front of the mustered troops. Once a soldier has made their legally protected decision of conscience, she or he can no longer be compelled by the German Armed Forces to execute any orders involving the use of arms. From that point on, they have the guaranteed right to a "conscience-sparing service alternative."

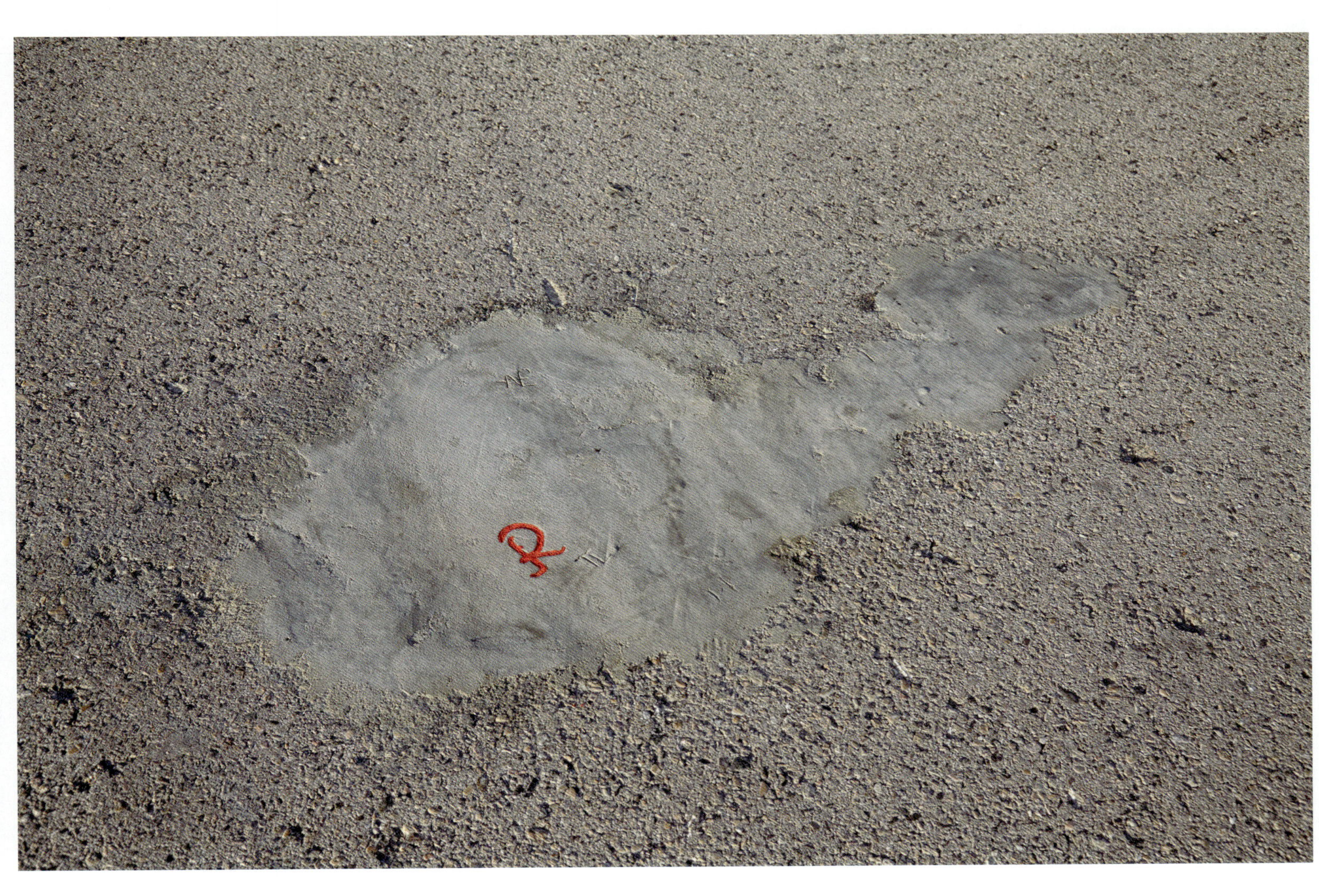

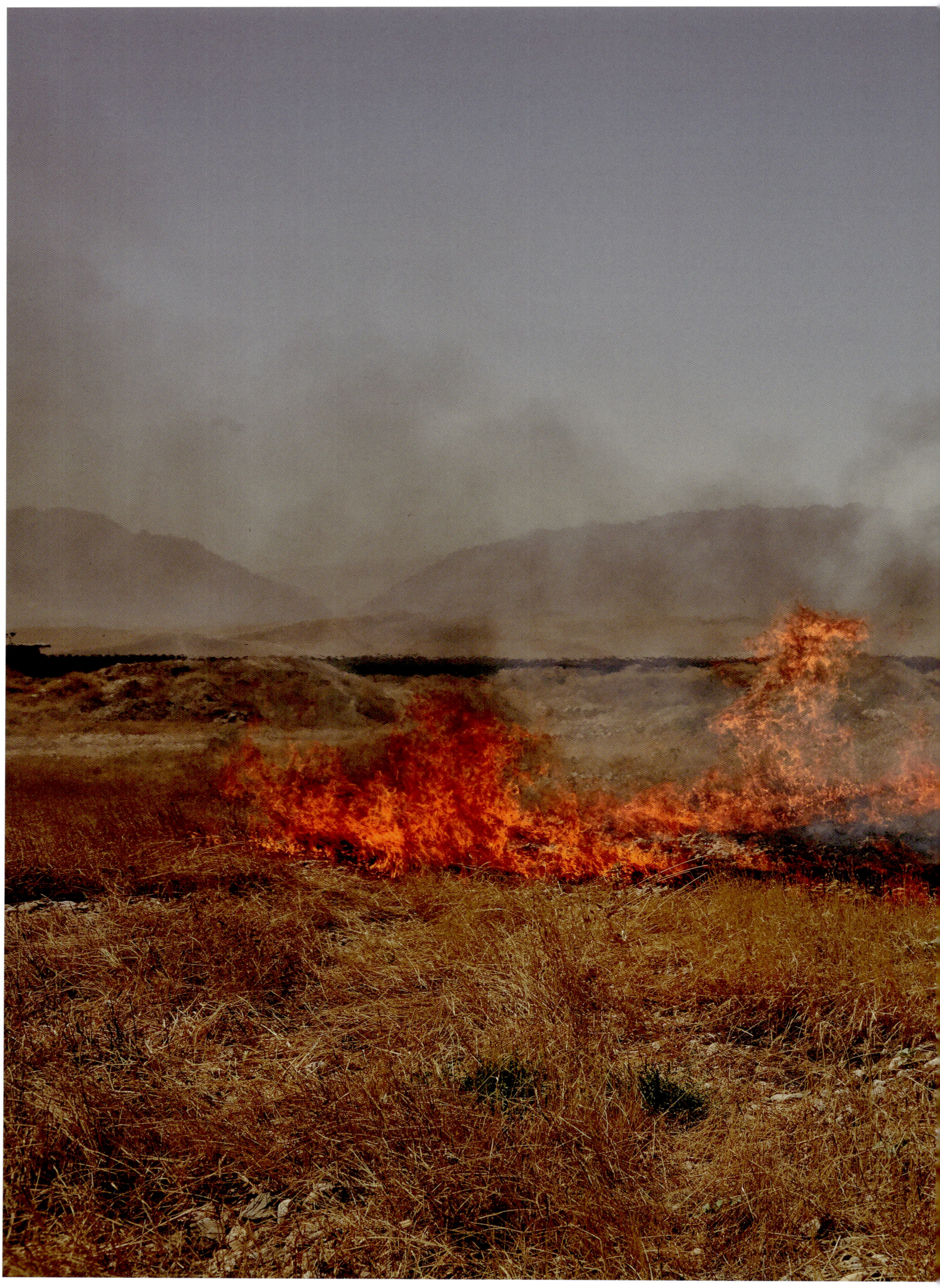

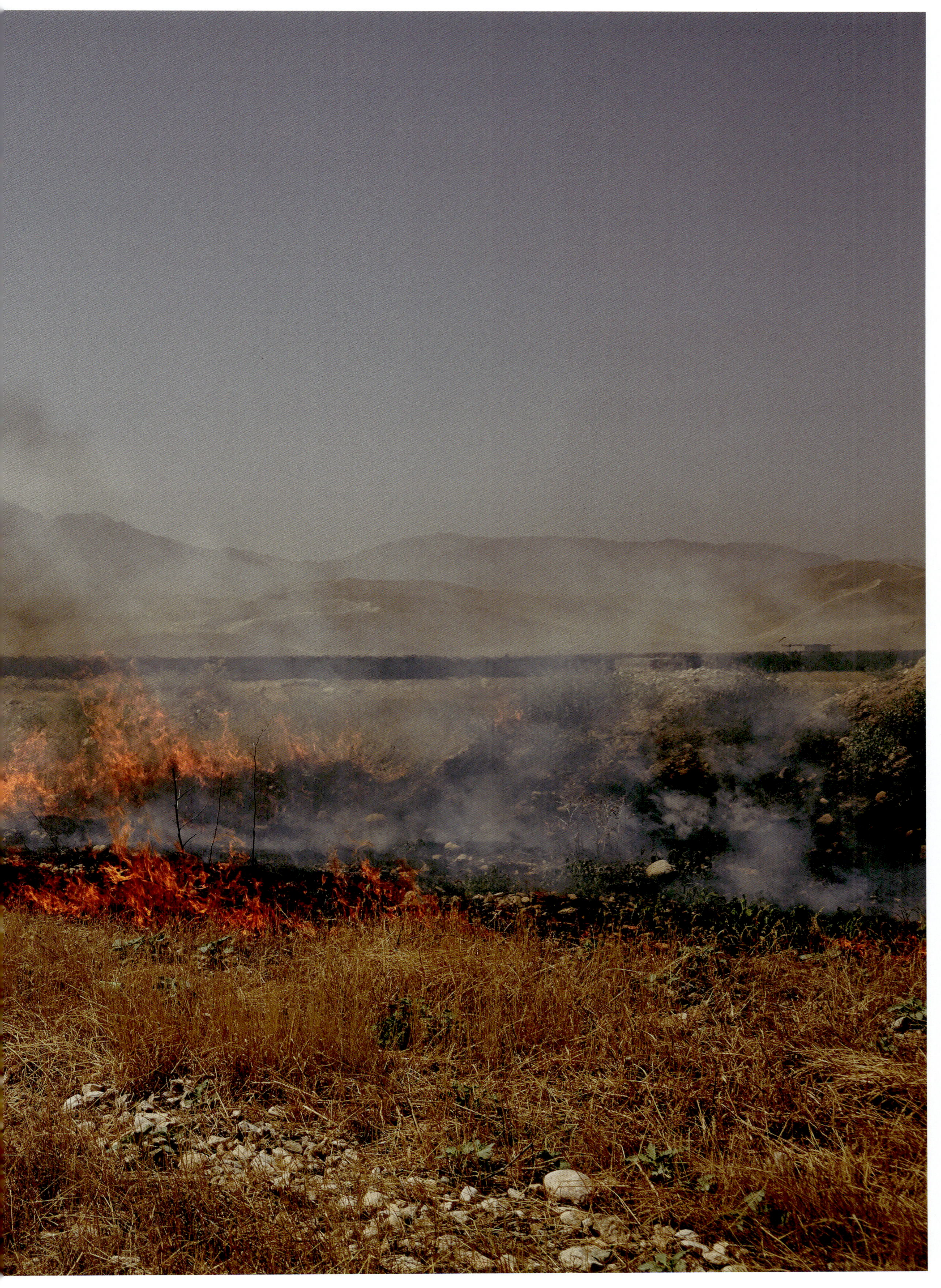

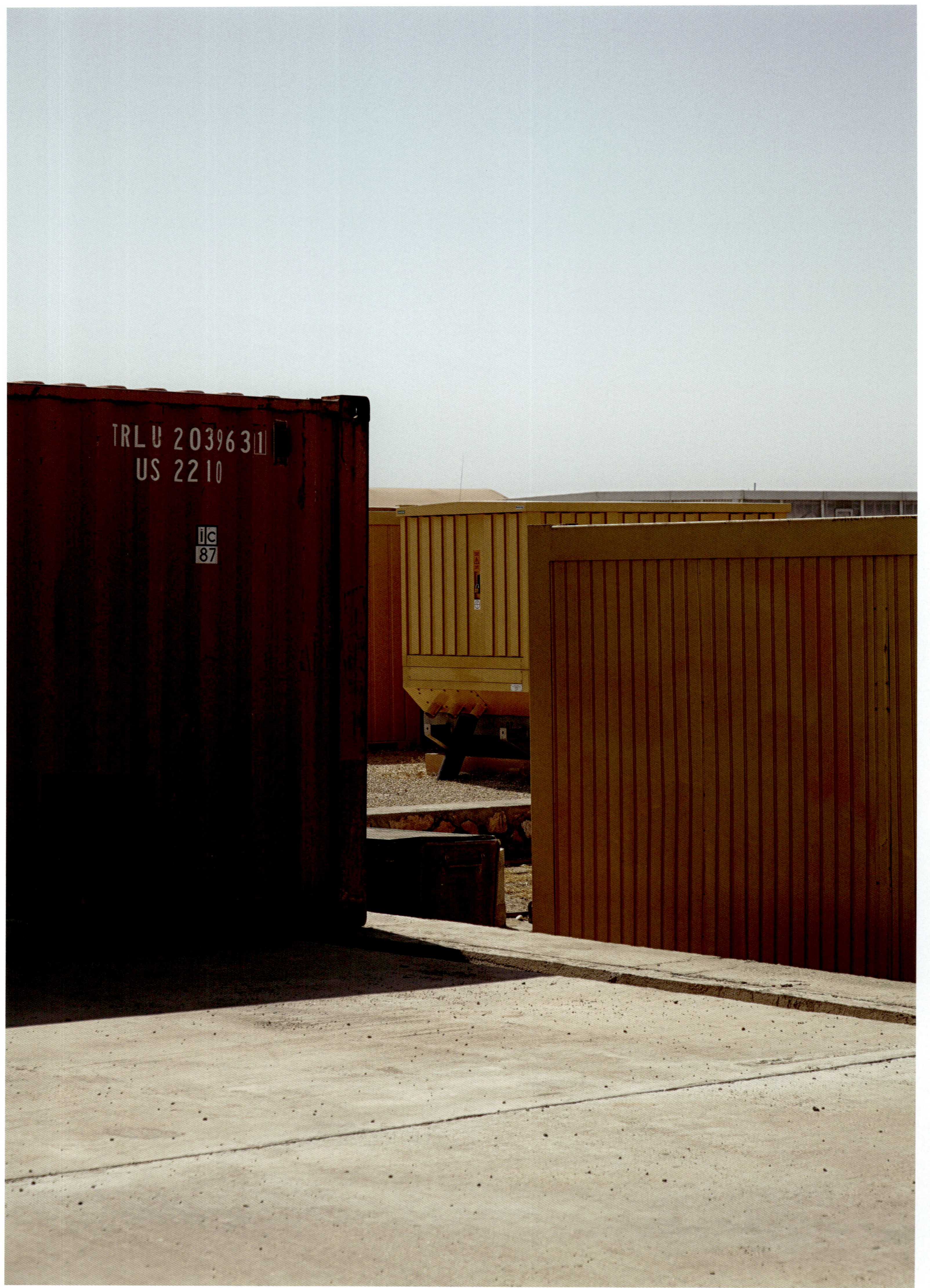

TRLU 203963 1
US 2210
IC
87

The two-member staff of the German Forces' Press and Public Relations Department work in a container-housed office in the camp headquarters. They distinguish themselves from one another in rank as superior and subordinate, as master and underling or, in the universal lingo of the camp, as 'Chief' and 'Administrator.' For the Chief of the Press Department, images are of the utmost importance. In his view, nothing exceeds the power of visual communication. To this end, a hydraulic man-lift is ordered over to the memorial for fallen soldiers on one of the few windy days of the summer. Standing on the platform of the man-lift, the Chief of the Press Department has himself hoisted above the memorial grounds so that he can secure a powerful image of the German flag fluttering against this background for the troops' homepage. All the while, the Administrator of the Press Department stands in the gravel below at the edge of the memorial grounds, an expression of admiration on his face as he gazes up to his colleague of higher position.

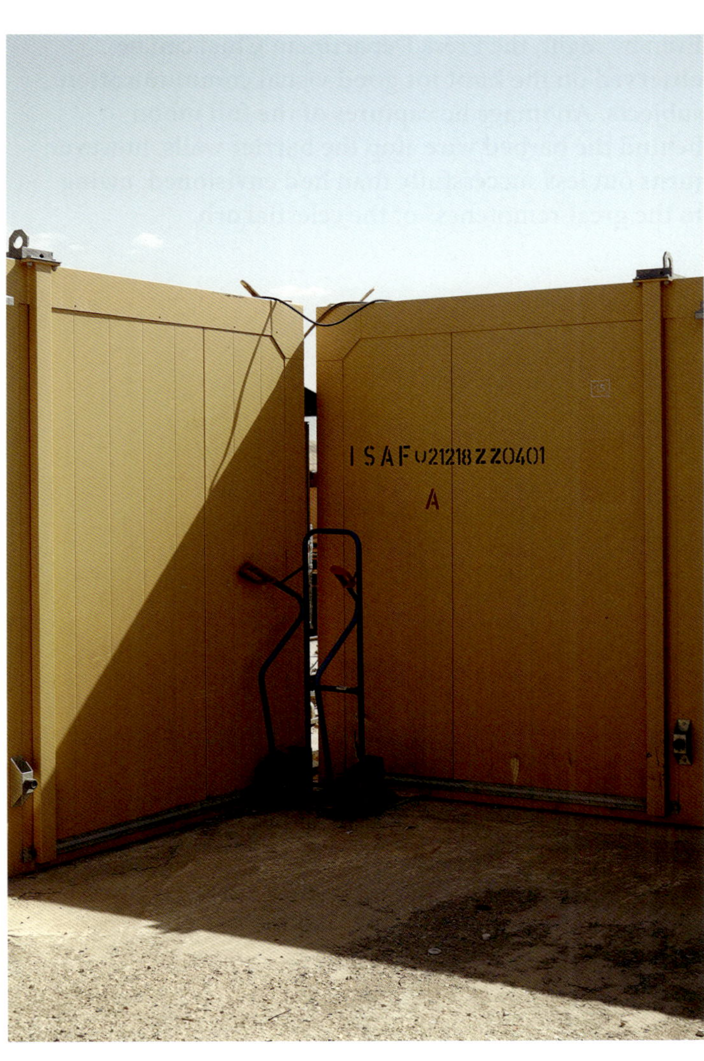

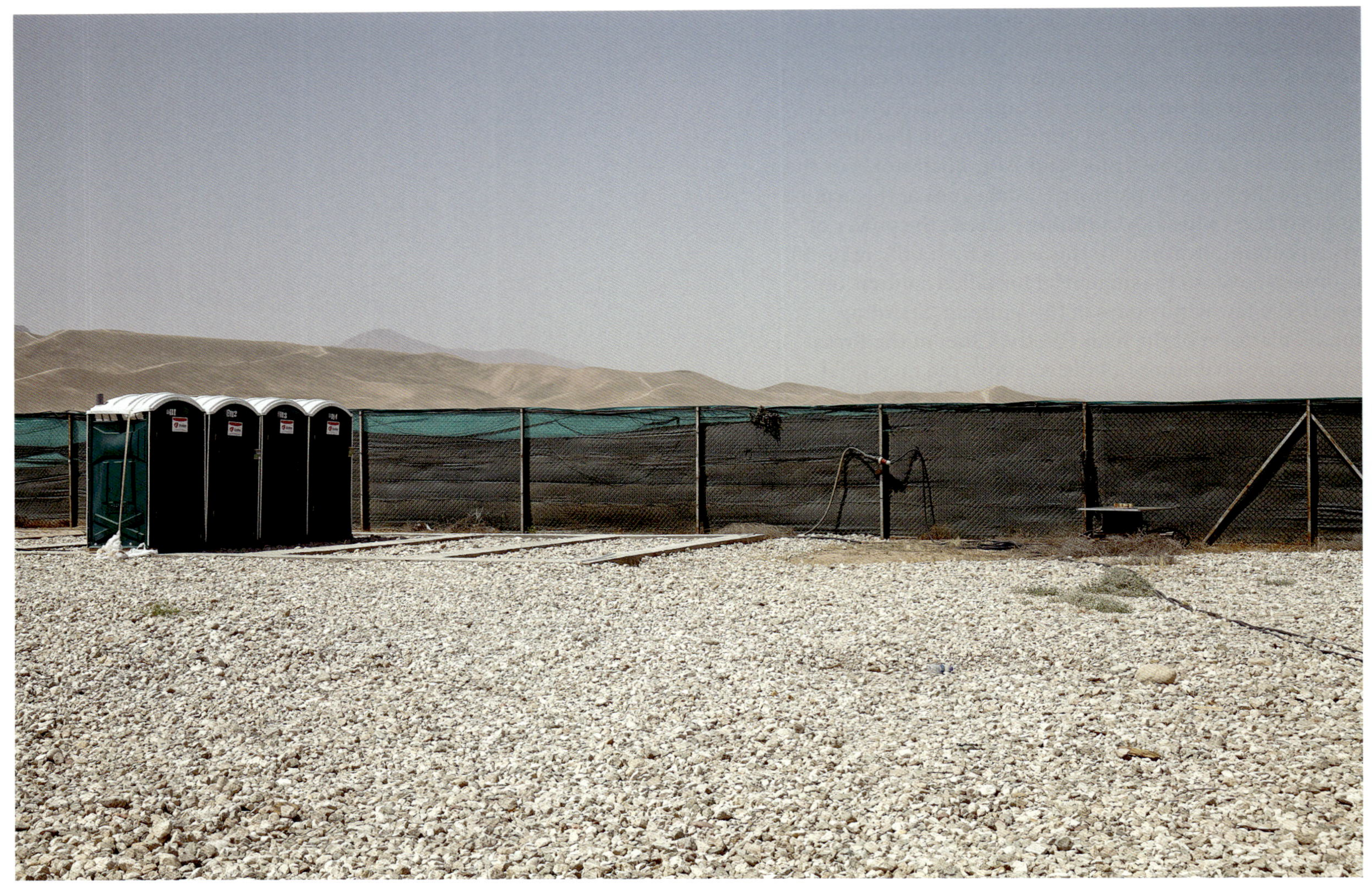

Even by night, the Press Department Chief can be
observed on the hunt for good visual communication
subjects. An image he captures of the full moon
behind the barbed wire atop the barrier walls, however,
turns out less successfully than he'd envisioned, owing
to the great remoteness of the celestial orb.

[320]

[324]

For many, life and work in the camp represents a form
of simplicity that would never be attainable in their
lives and work outside of the camp. For the duration of
their deployment, the complexity of everyday life and
its demands is streamlined and structured. There is
certainty about the course of the day's events, about when
to eat and when to rest, about duties and official channels,
associations with fellow soldiers, the limits of their own
authority and of the space they have in which to live.
The interpretation and classification of events and the
implications they have for strategic planning in the immediate future are the responsibility of mission command.
Anyone who has prior experience with life in the camp
already knows upon arrival where everything is and
how things work. For only a very few do any issues remain
unresolved for the handful of months that they spend
there.

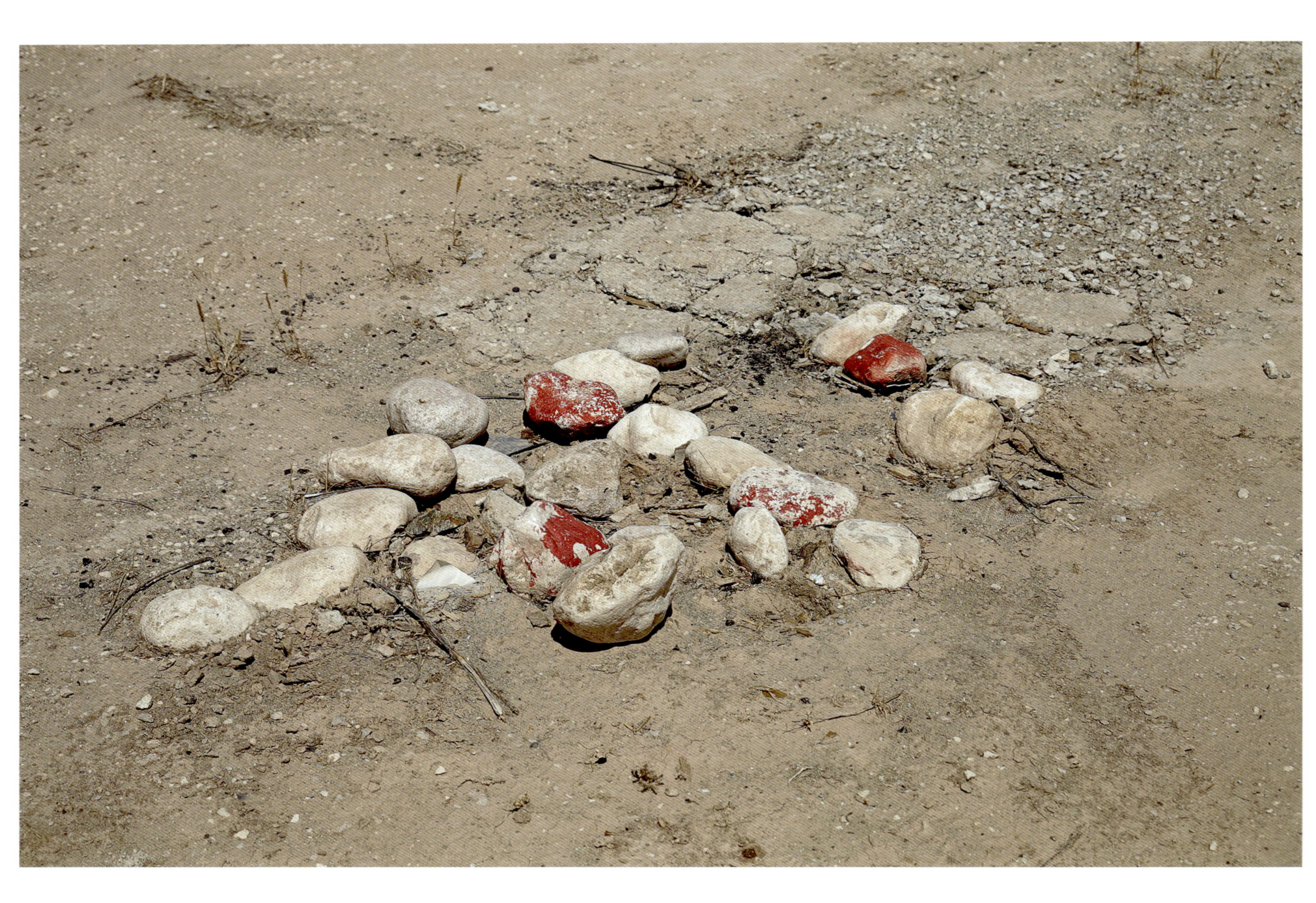

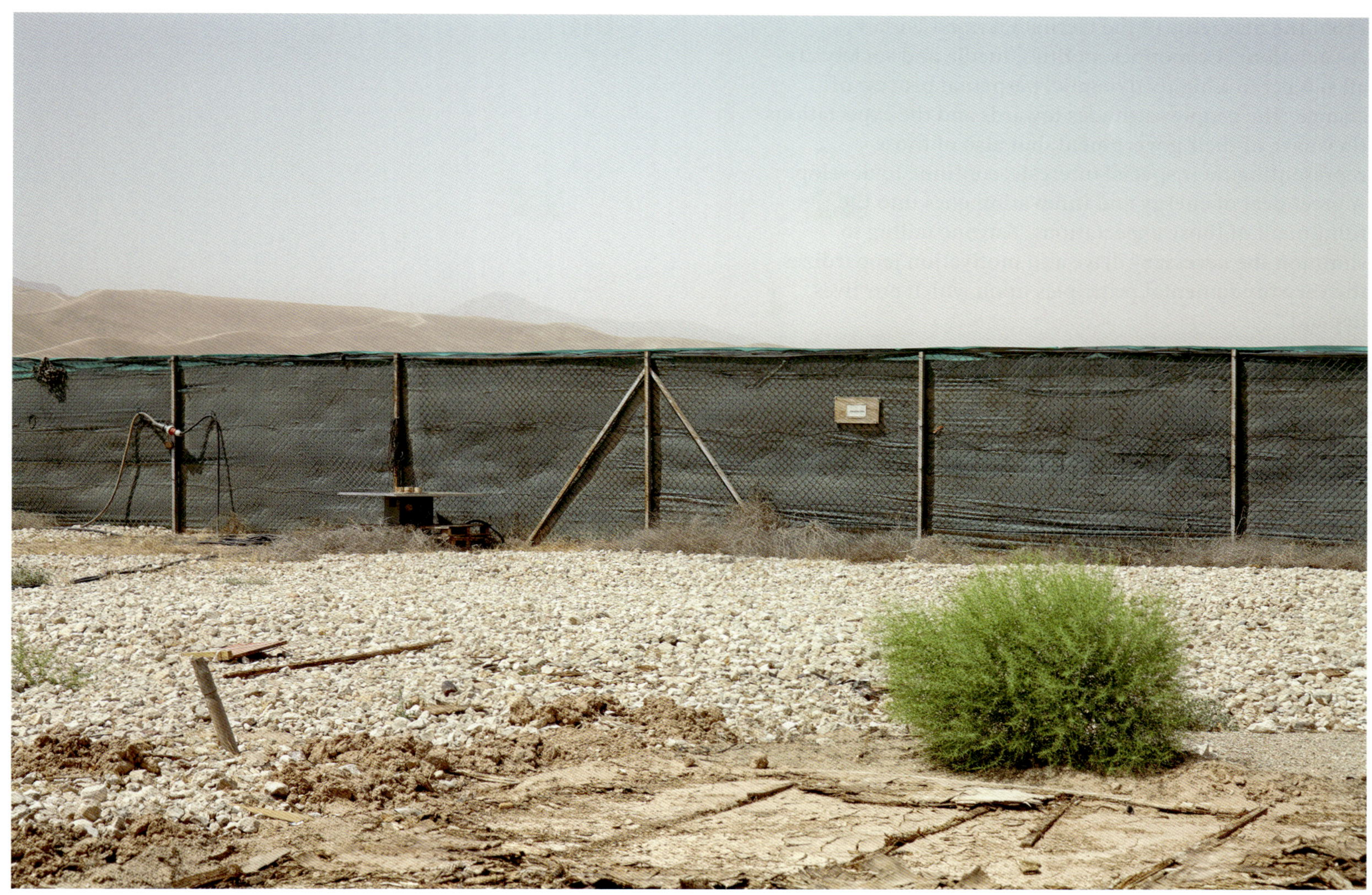

After returning home, many suffer from a kind of
repatriation depression, due in no small part to the sudden
incursion of life's complexity into their daily routines.
For many, even the past deployment, in its perceived
simplicity and its explication and regulation of all external
concerns, appears in hindsight to be a matter of extra-
ordinary complexity. The biggest problem, though, is to
hear First Sergeant P. tell it, is that after their time in the
camp, the reality at home seems alien, and they soon
long for the routines which for months have governed their
daily lives.

[332]

[334]

[335]

[336]

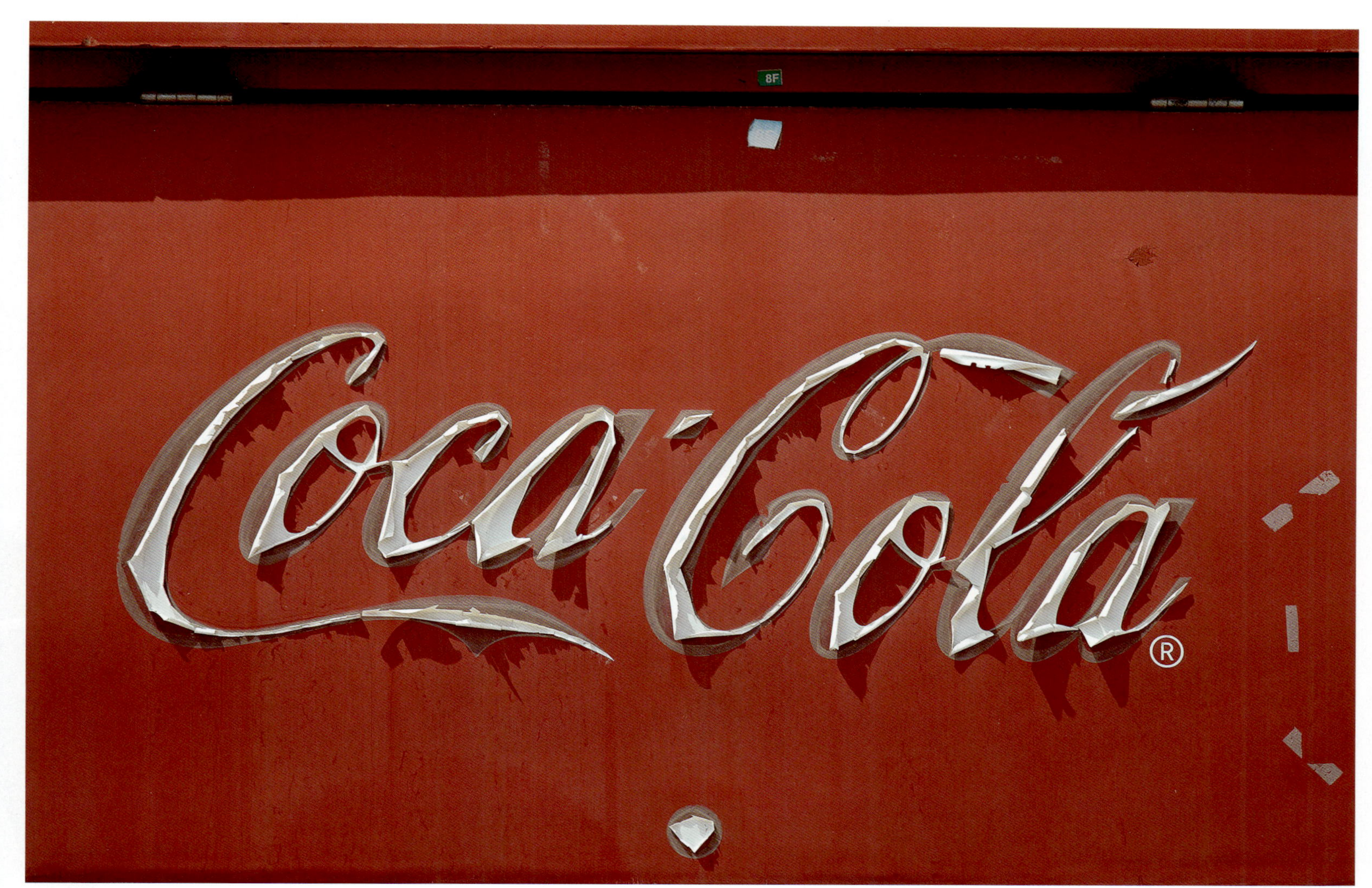

Foremost quality of a soldier: patience.   [340]

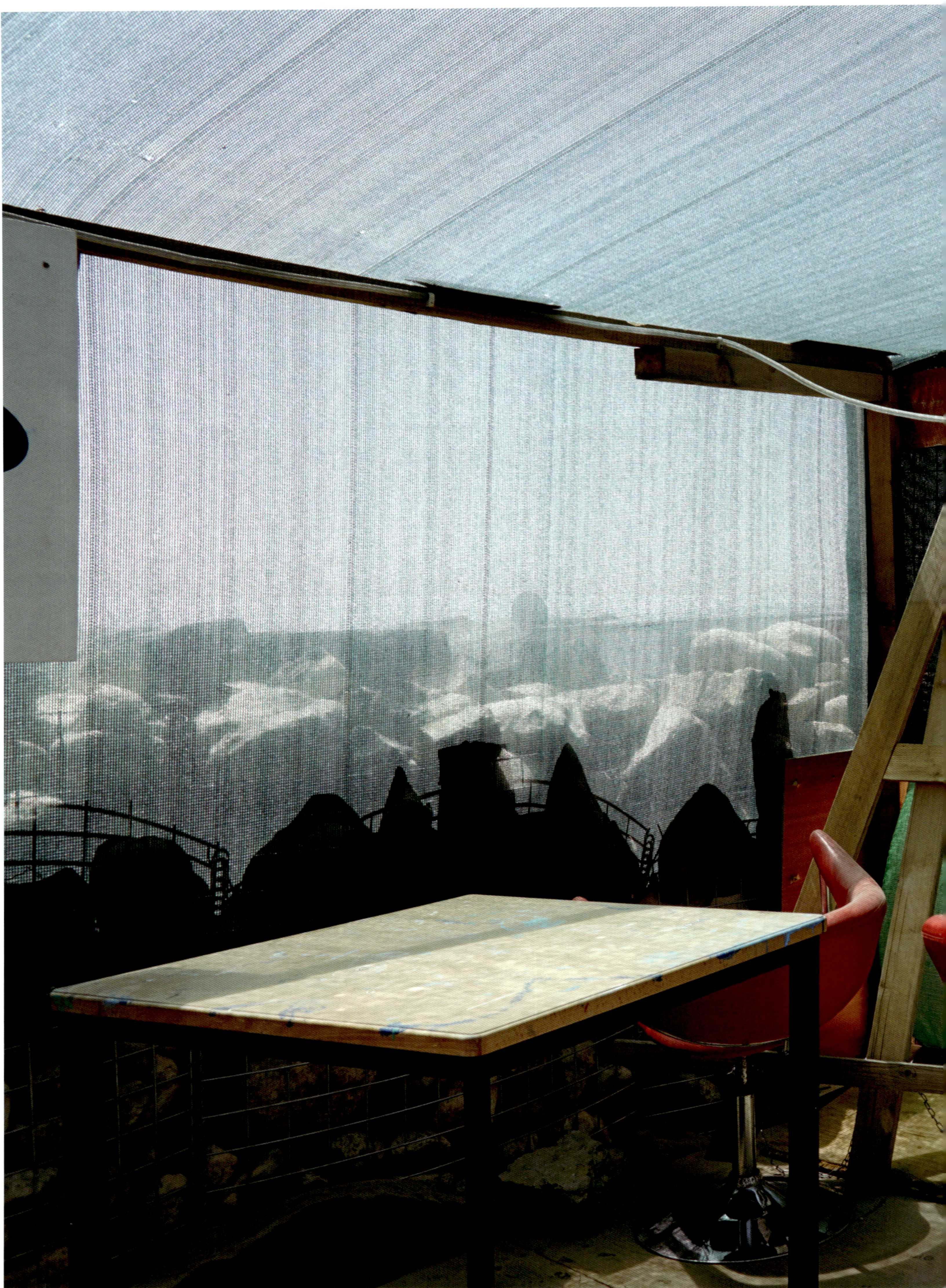

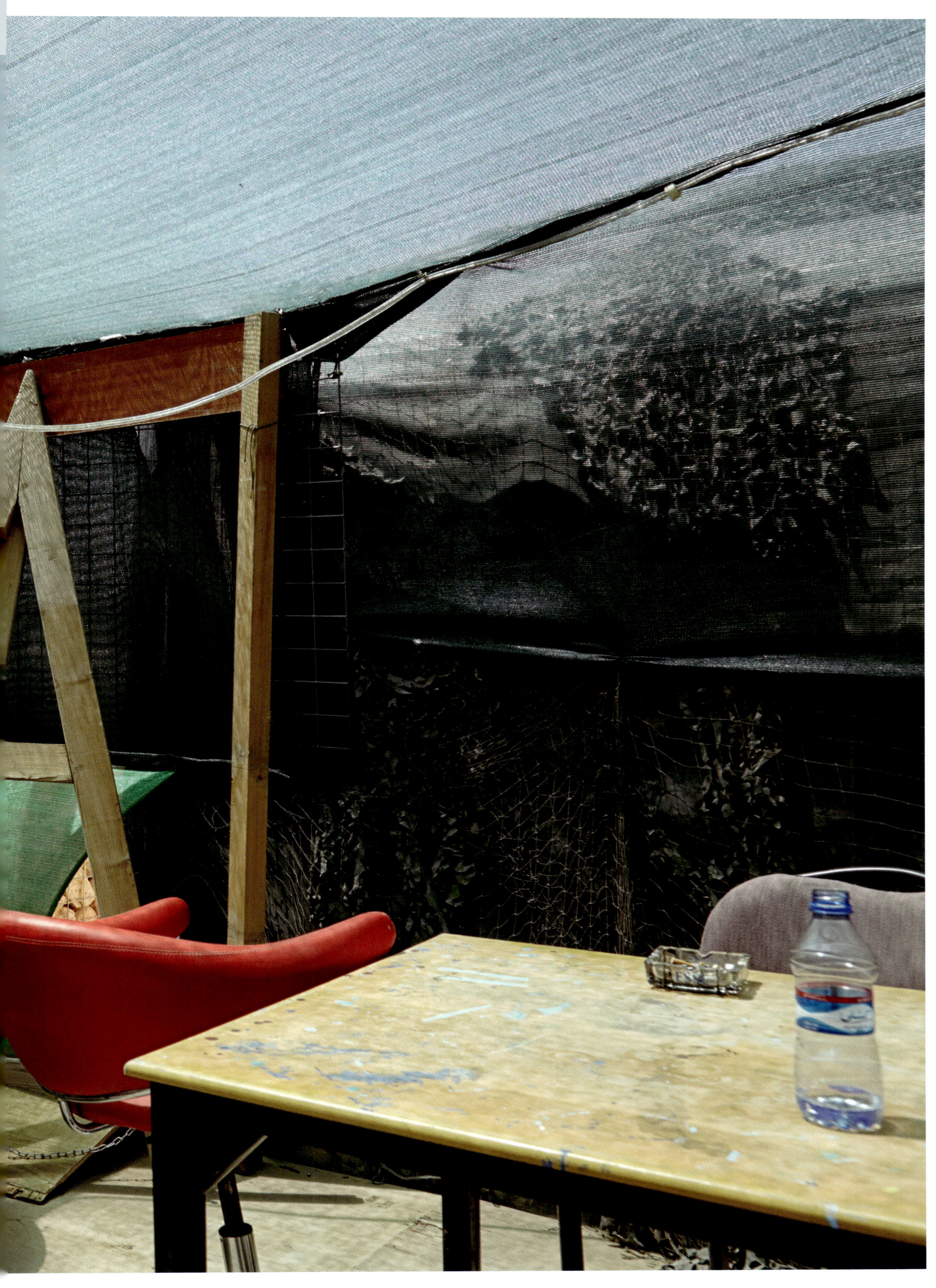

[349]

Concrete drainage channels have been installed alongside each and every roadway running through the camp.
At this time of year they're mostly dry; in spring they carry away the water from the mountains as the snow melts and the brief rainy season begins. In the course of a single day, a small creek has formed in one of these channels due to a large volume of water having been pumped from the camp's internal drinking water wells for maintenance reasons. In no time at all, a number of frogs appear in the little stream, and a pink rubber ball bobs alongside the road on its surface.

Not long before this, the advisory had been issued to shower no more than once per day and for no longer than four minutes at a time. Also under consideration had been the temporary closure of the sports and fitness facilities, in order to prevent soldiers who had already used up their bathing water allowance in the morning from getting under the shower again in the evening after working out.

[352]

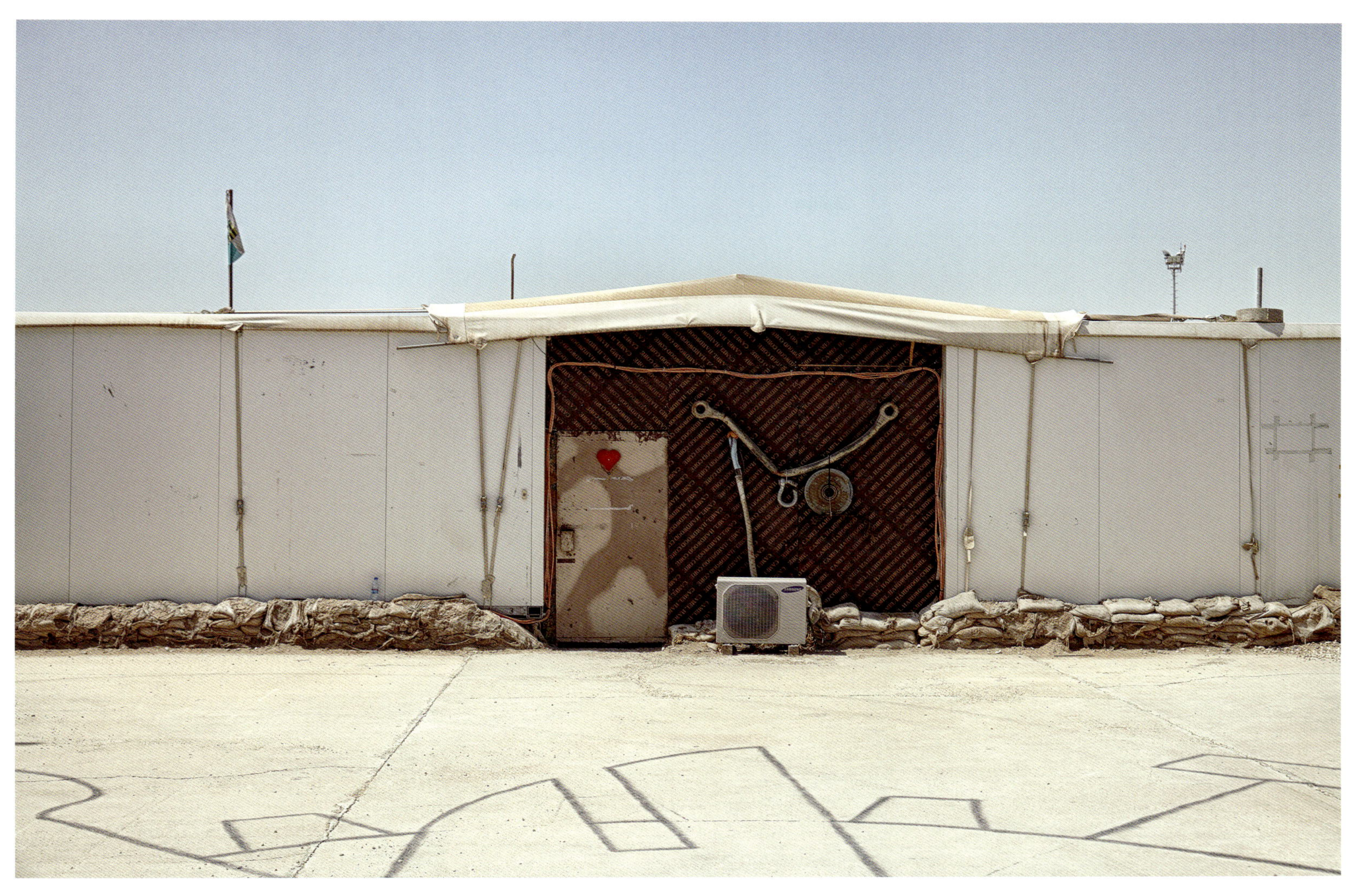

The grey Airbus plane with the insignia of the German Air Force on its side hardly differs from any ordinary commercial airliner. The flight attendants may be wearing green jumpsuits, but the in-flight meals they serve bear the logo of Lufthansa. There is no First Class. One can look down the entire length of the passenger cabin to the door of the cockpit, which most of the time stays open.

For its landing in the camp, the grey passenger plane is joined by an escort of two fighter jets. Additionally, the window shades are drawn down, and the aircraft completely darkened. The orange glow of the fasten seat-belt signs is the sole remaining light source in the cabin. The passengers, most of whom are in uniform, their faces devoid of expression, sit motionless in this droning, darkened tube for the entire duration of the landing descent into camp. Every so often the cabin shudders and one thinks: this is it. But the time stretches out long before the plane actually touches down on the landing strip. The passengers stand up and exit in a controlled, orderly manner, stepping out of the plane and into the likewise orange glow of the airport lighting. The arrivals area contains a garage-like corrugated metal hangar, hung inside with camouflage netting and flags. There are foosball tables for the people waiting and seating accommodation made of bamboo. A great many soldiers have come to greet the new arrivals. There's a lot of hugging and clapping one another on the shoulder. Several of the soldiers who've gathered to welcome the others are sporting full beards.

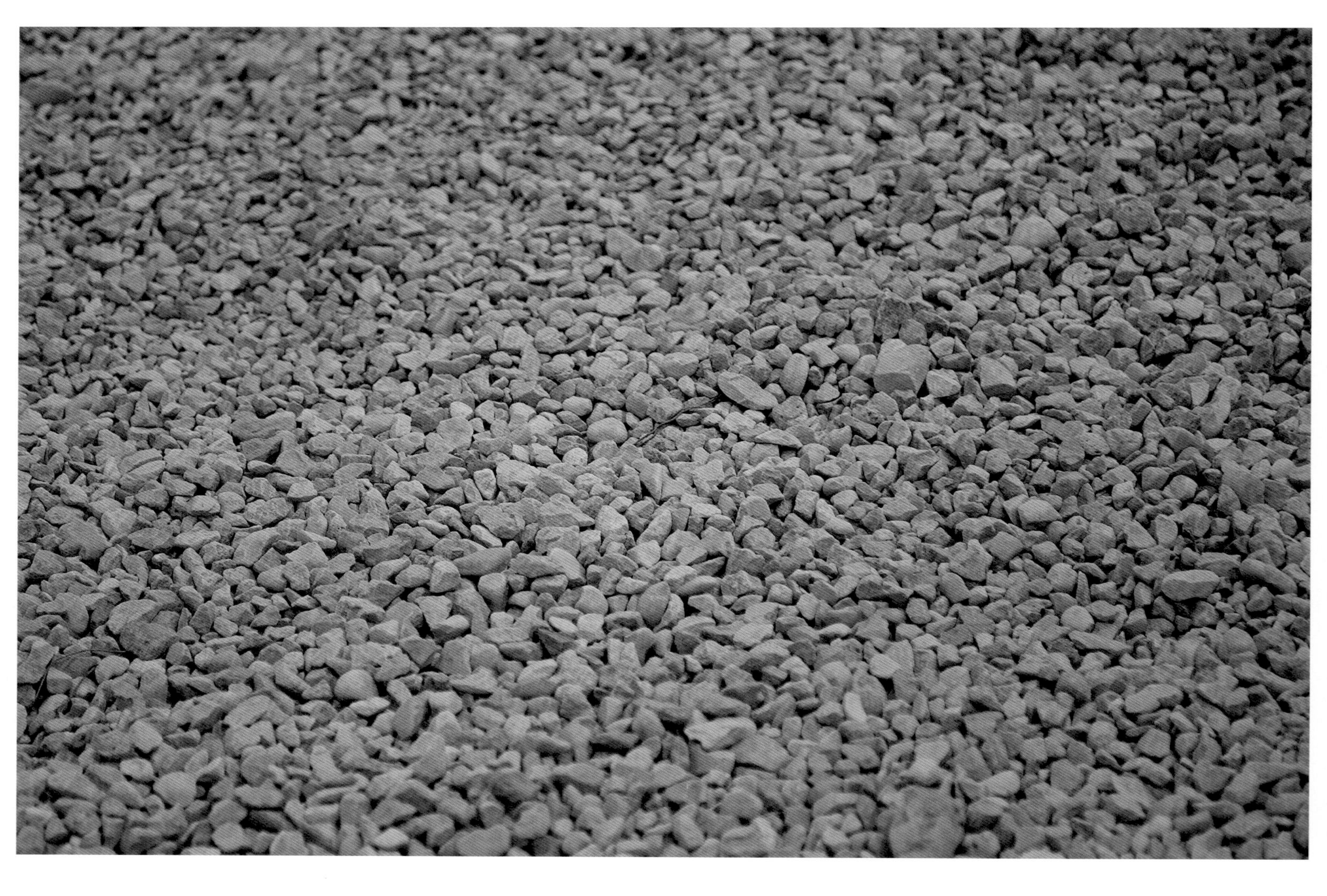

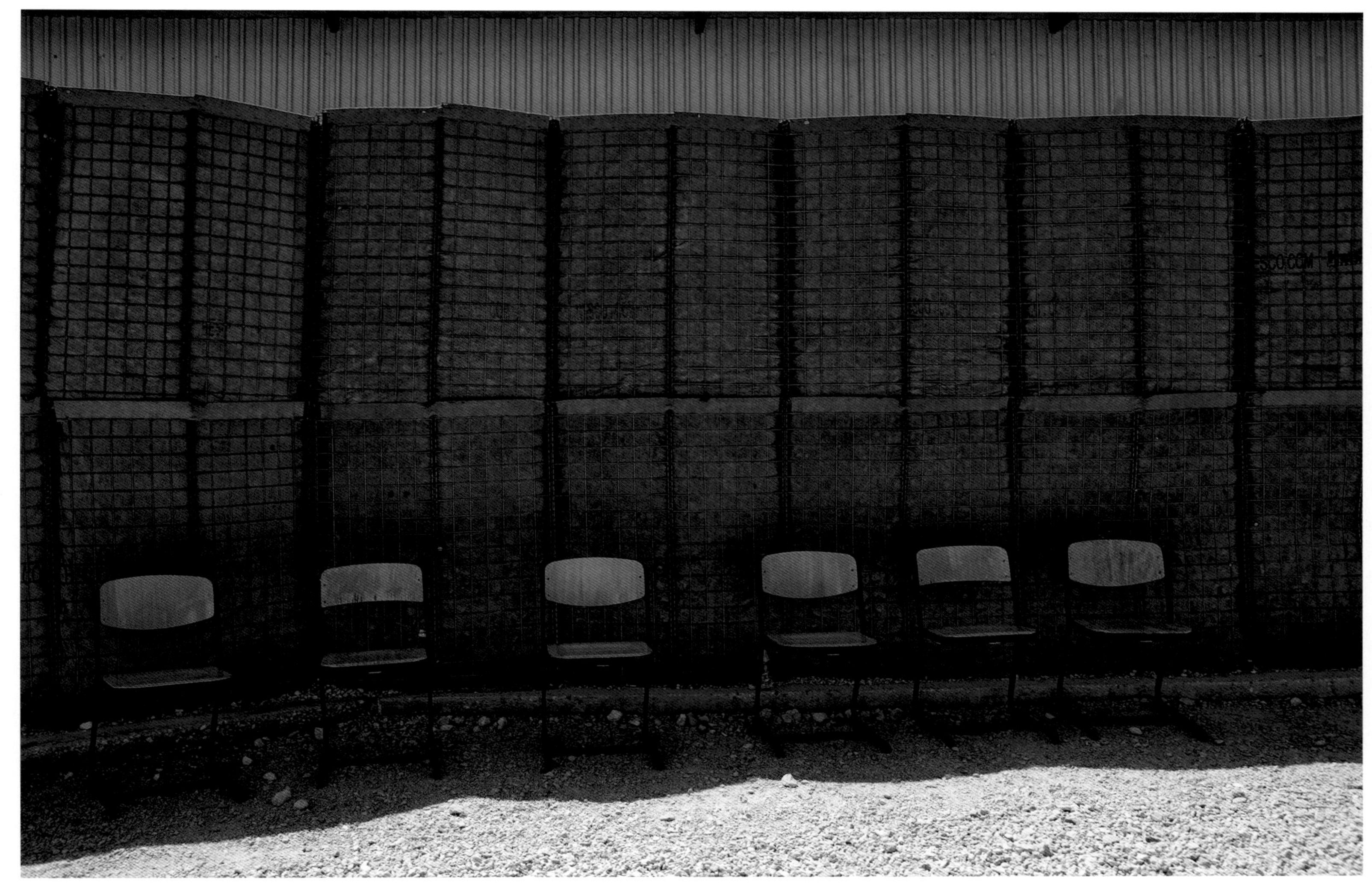

On the wall of the camp commander's container hang framed portraits of Joachim Gauck, Angela Merkel, and Ursula von der Leyen. Across from the massive desk, a synthetic leather sofa and set of matching chairs are arranged around a glass coffee table. A lower-ranking soldier brings in ice-cold cans of soda on a tray. The Commanding General is talking about how they'd intended to leave behind a "light footprint" in this country. As camp commander, he says, he's really just another soldier on deployment, albeit one appointed by the Minister of Defense. During his camp radio appearance a few minutes before, he called for having patience with the local workers, as their month of fasting was coming up, and considering the regional climate conditions, they would be under enormous strain. He then saluted all of the soldiers with the Pink Floyd song "Wish You Were Here."

Leadership and building faith in the mission are foremost among his duties, says the General. The point is to convey to the soldiers the feeling that they're putting their lives on the line for a good cause. After all, he says, the army, if nothing else, is a community of shared values predicated on consensus. On the surface, you have to be able to appear threatening. But the General sees the basis for his work in the superbly functioning democracy of his native Germany. And this, he says, is his own country's most formidable weapon. When asked if perhaps it would be alright to take a photo of his office, the General answers: "Fire away!"

A security checkpoint manned by Armenian soldiers
leads from the road to the taxiway of the military airbase
in the camp. The airbase shares its take-off and landing
strips with the civilian airport that serves the neighboring
city. If someone wants to pass through this checkpoint
with a car, they must first get out and go around picking
all of the little rocks out of the car's tire treads, as these
little rocks pose a hazard for the airplanes' turbines.
From the taxiway, one crosses the take-off and landing
strips and finds themselves without further ado on the
grounds of the civilian airport. A newly built arrival hall
stands there as if abandoned. Oversize portraits of the
country's highest-ranking politicians hang from the façade;
their's are the only faces to be seen anywhere in the
vicinity. Turkish Airlines offers regular flights between
the nearby city and Istanbul, but the flight times are
sporadic. Only a very small fraction of the population can
afford to travel by air.

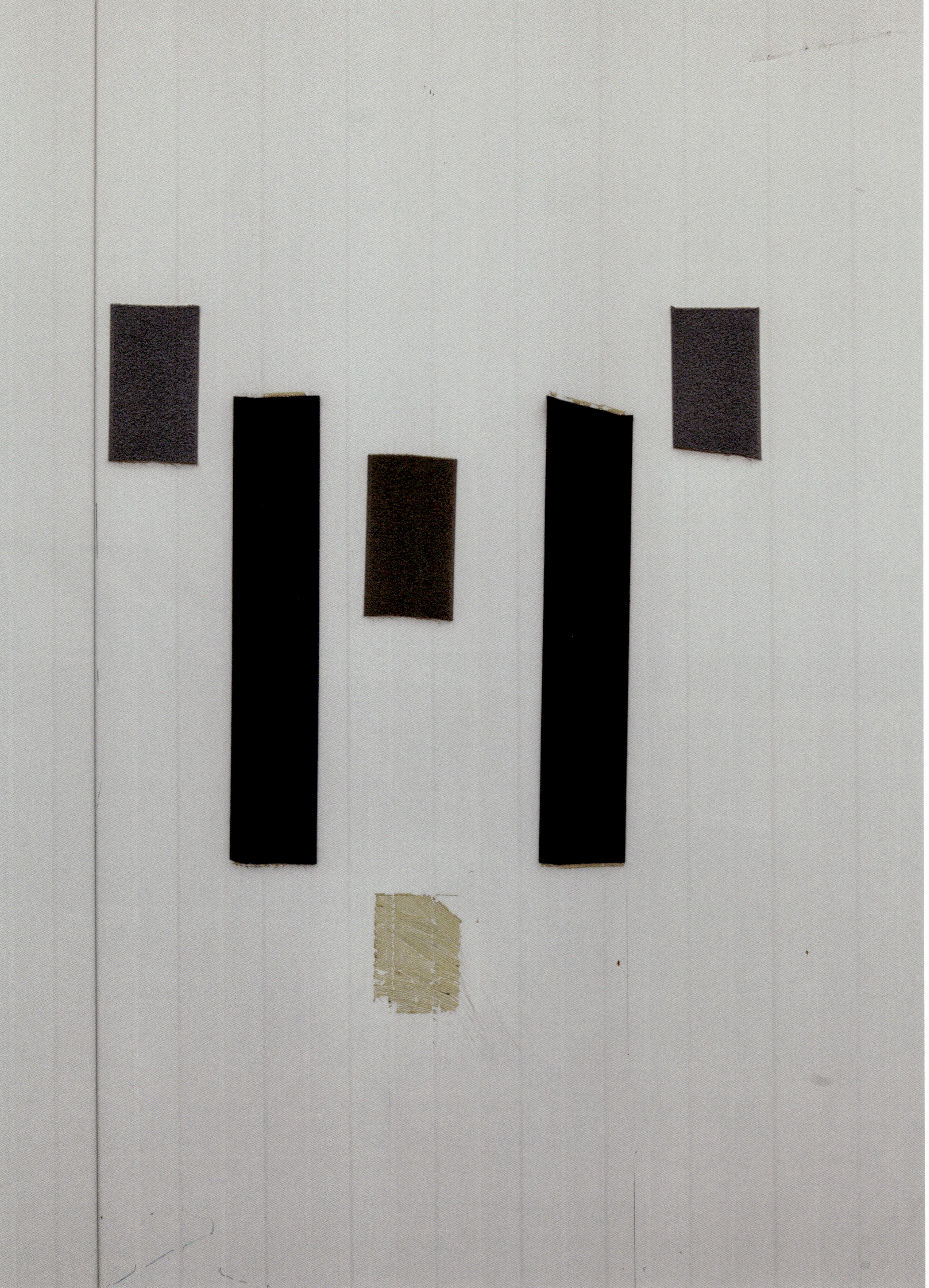

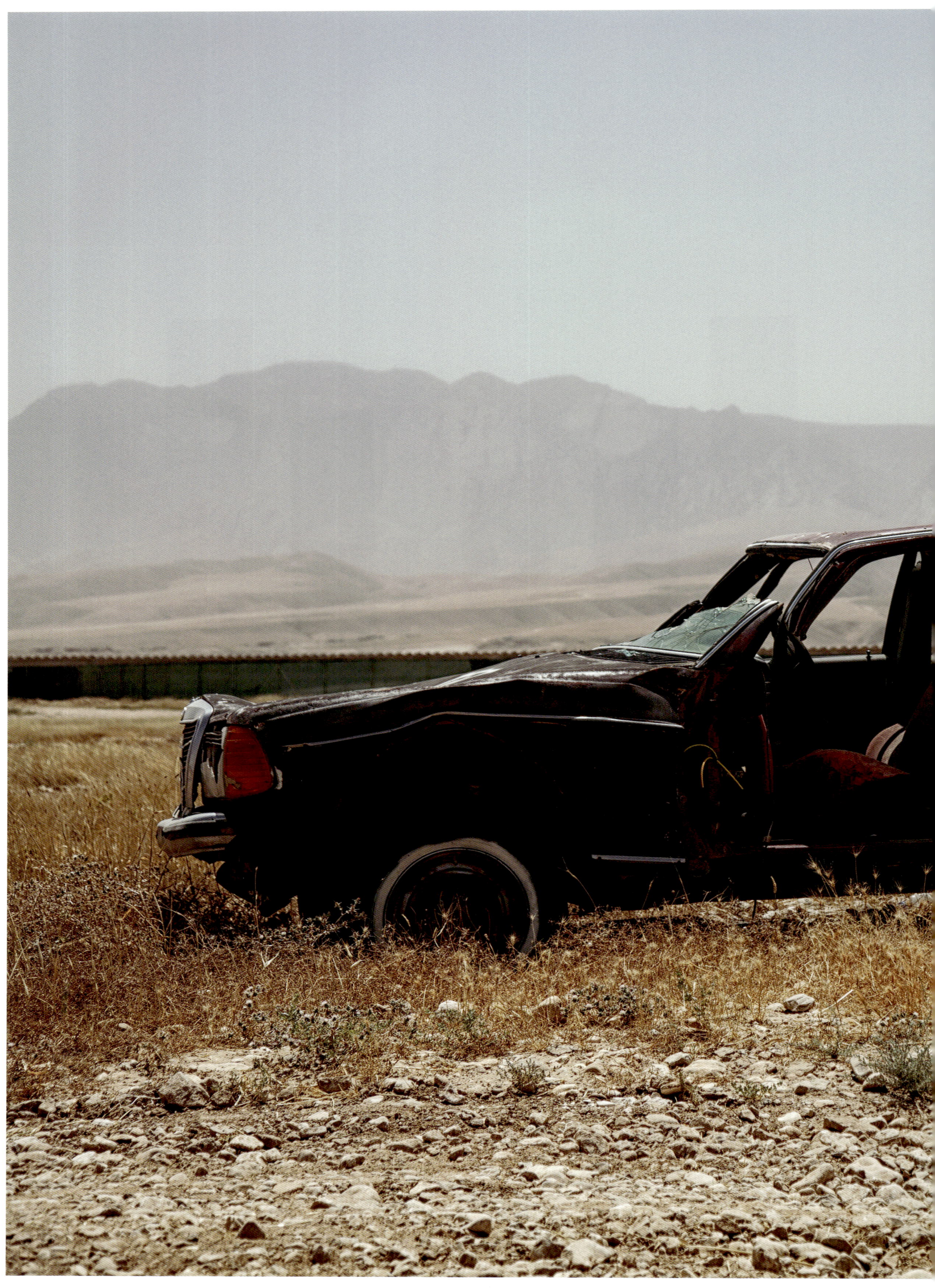

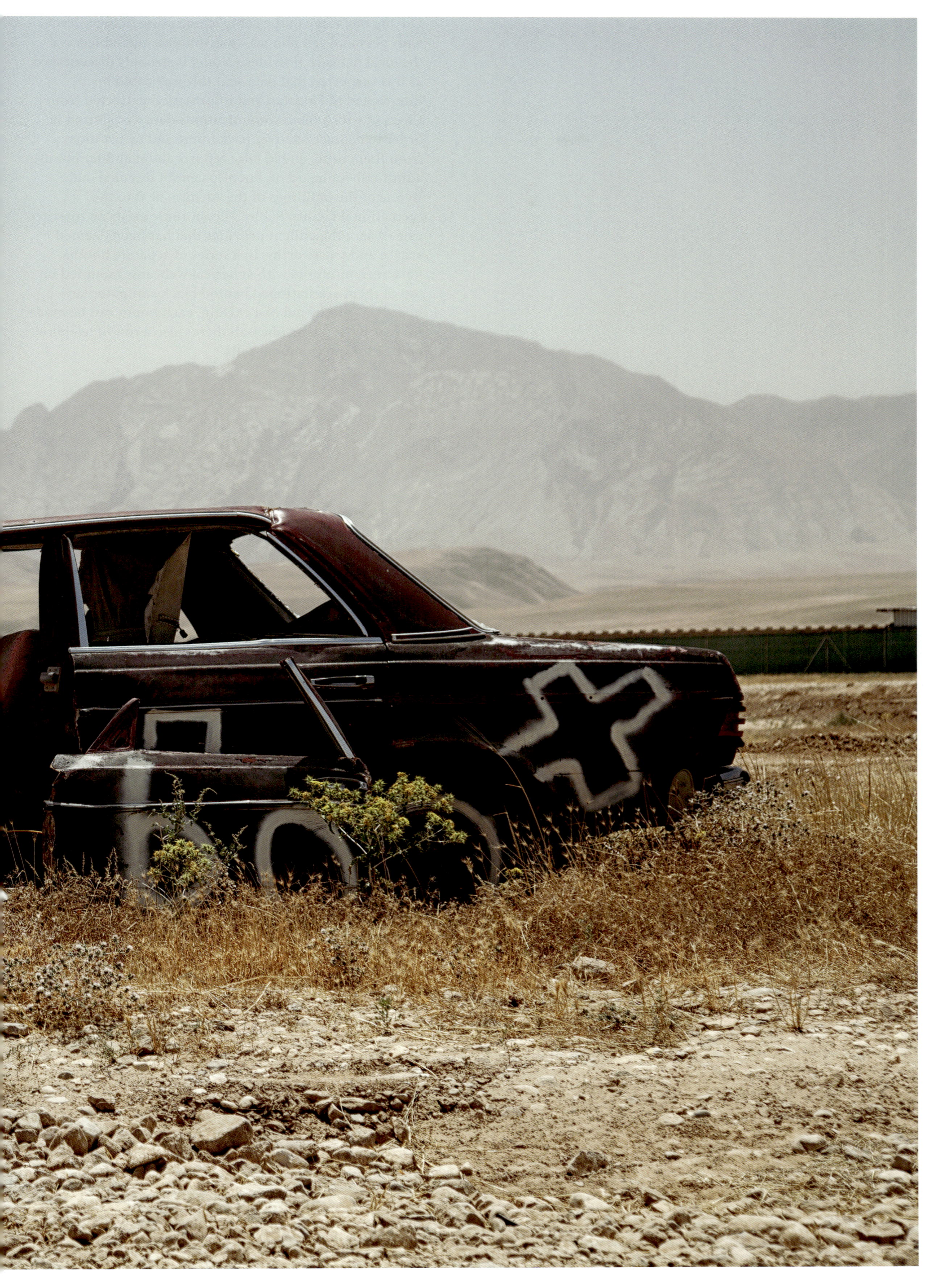

During one's stay in the camp, connecting to the internet with personal cell phones, smartphones and tablets via the local network provider *Etisalat* is strongly discouraged, as it is suspected that data sent this way could be intercepted in Pakistan and information extracted from it. Cases in which telecommunications data was abused in order to contact relatives back home and extort money from them or to spread false reports about abductions are admittedly unheard of, but also cannot be ruled out.
In one of the buildings of the Atrium, next to the recreational facility *Planet Mazar*, there exists an internet café of an independent provider that has been deemed secure and trustworthy. In a series of separate booths, flatscreen monitors with spherical webcams mounted on top of them are stationed behind black computer keyboards. With the aid of a curtain, each booth can be made more private. Along one wall there's also a row of telephone booths for international calls.

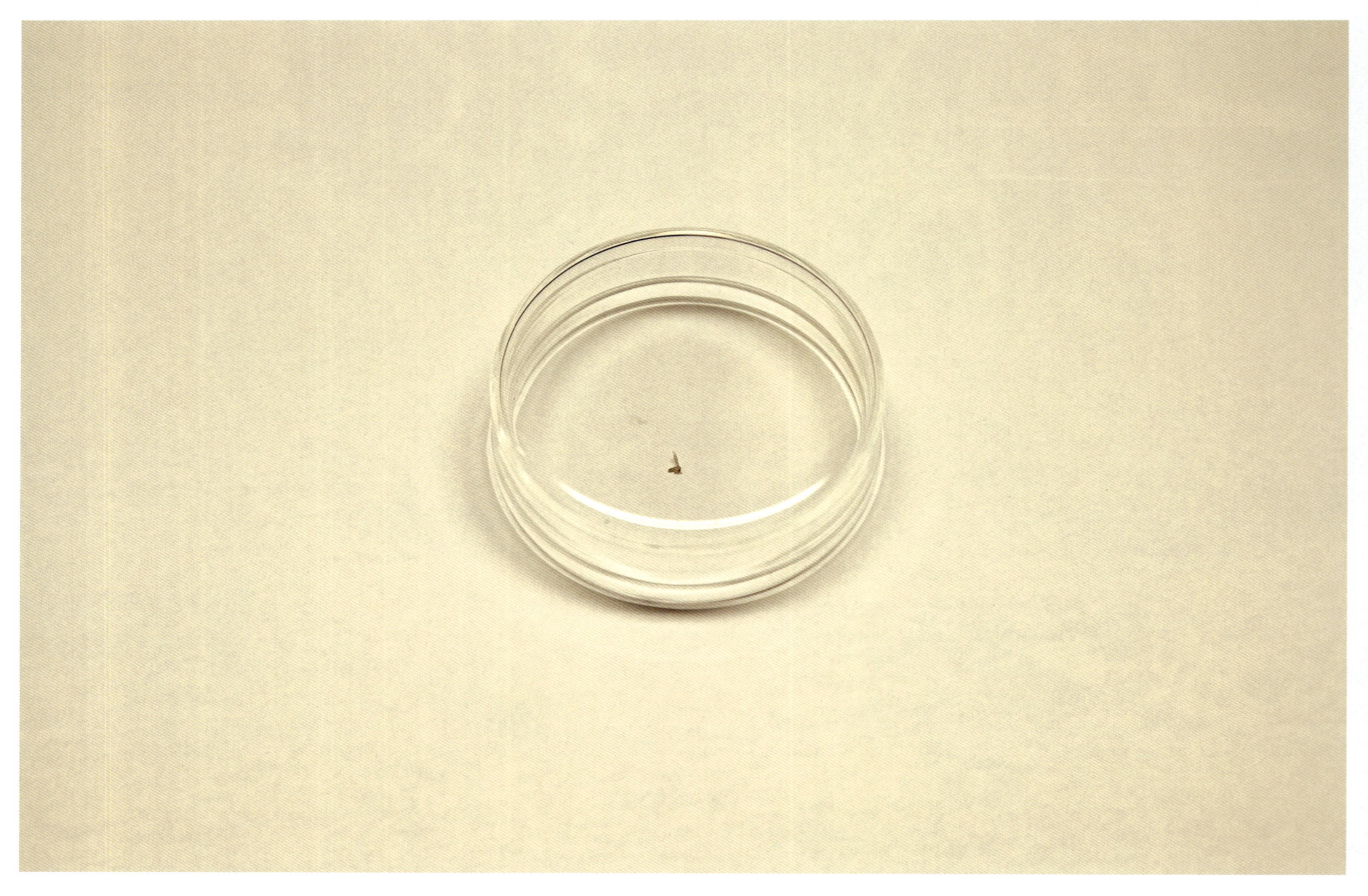

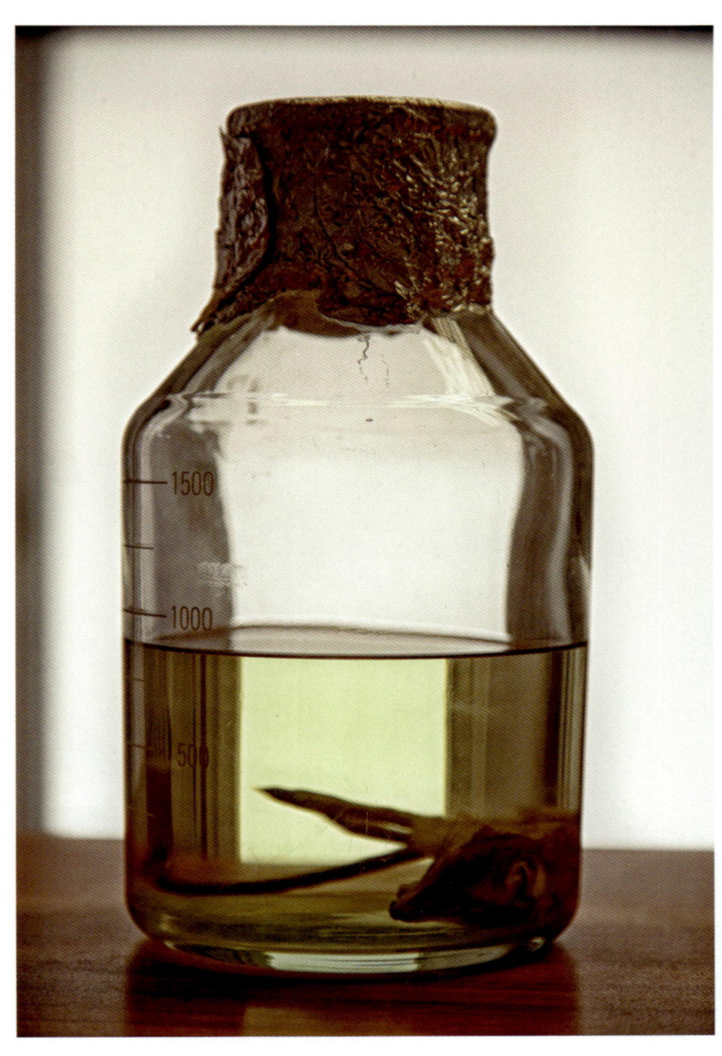

At all hours of the day or night, the internet café is utterly deserted. Nowadays no one uses these computers behind the curtains drawn neatly to one side. The lights remain on and the air conditioning running, and at several of the stations, pairs of dice dance or series of words undulate across the screens. Anyone from *Planet Mazar* needing to use the restroom passes by the vacant internet café. On the walls hang posters of frigates, warplanes, helicopters, and beaches in the Caribbean. It's as if the café is suspended in permanent anticipation of all those who in the past, prior to the invention of the mobile internet, once came here to connect with their relatives, friends, wives, and husbands. Despite the supposed risks, however, the soldiers stationed in the camp now prefer to contact their loved ones in private on their personal devices. The café remains unused.

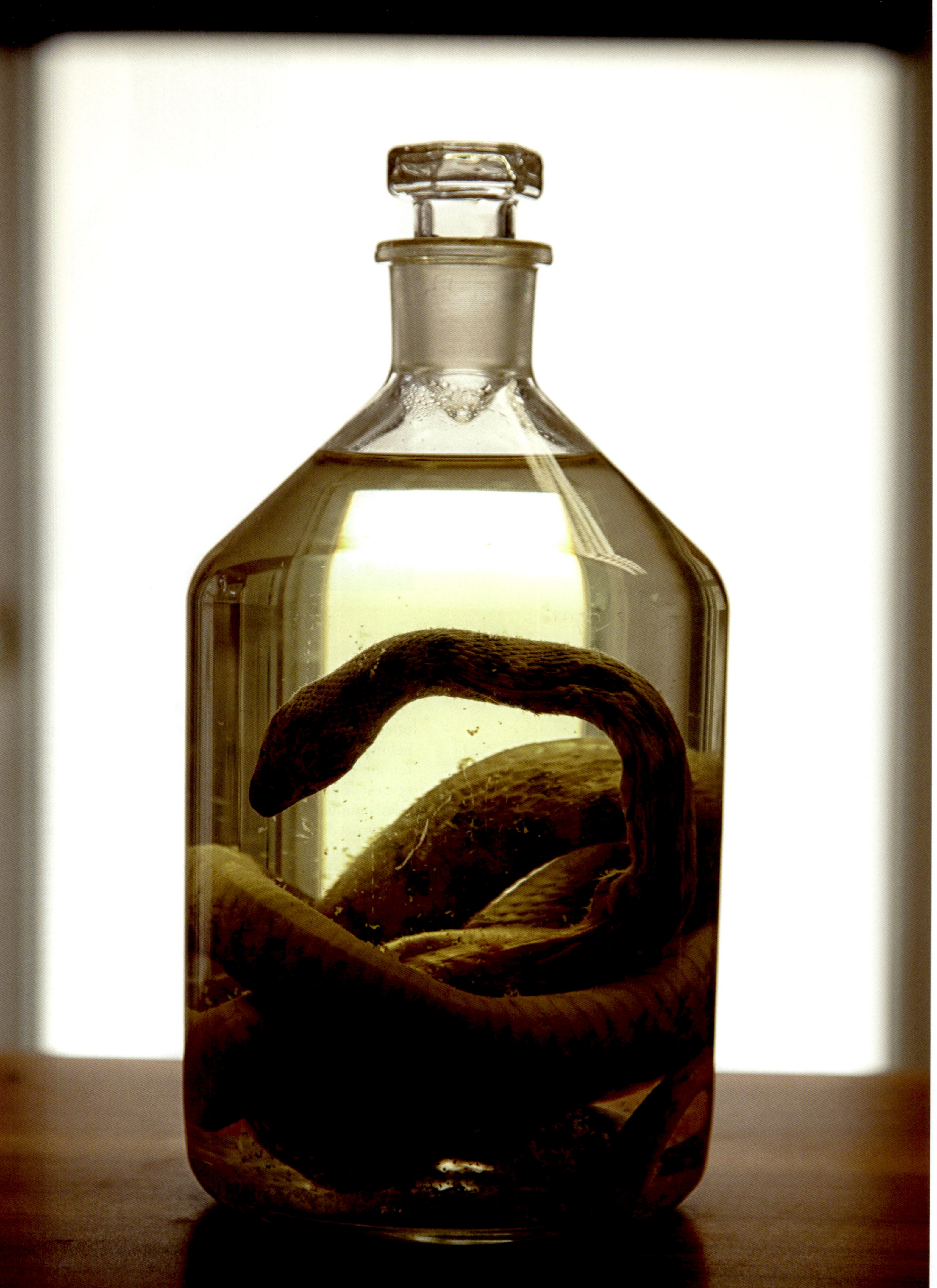

The way out of the camp leads through a series of various checkpoints and security zones beginning at the main gate. The local workers, security forces, and those few who regularly leave the camp as part of their training mission pass through these checkpoints and security zones multiple times a day. But for those who stay behind in the camp, this remains a rarity. Some of them know only in theory about the outer rings of security zones.

[394]

The Chief of the Press Department sets out in person through these checkpoints and security zones, through the Mongolian Gate, past the desk of the security guard on duty, through the cramped passageways that look like starting boxes at dog races in a covered area with grim-faced guards, past the massive x-ray apparatus that scans each vehicle coming in or out, through the narrow wire mesh corridors, past the anti-tank barriers and cement blocks, all the way to the Afghan Gate, where a few weary-looking soldiers have spread out some raffia mats in the shade of a tarp. In the intermediate area between the Mongolian and Afghan Gates are little sheds, like those found in community allotment gardens, ramshackle workshops in tents, decommissioned containers full of wooden slats and rusty rolls of wire. The Afghan Gate opens onto a road running alongside the camp wall.

[395]

[405]

In the Atrium's recreational facility *Planet Mazar*,
club music is played every night. There's a raised platform
for the DJ overlooking the dance floor, which for the most
part stays empty, if not for the occasional little groups
of soldiers standing there milling about and chatting with
one another. In the evening, at the edge of the dance floor,
video screens are lowered and scenes of half-naked people
dancing at foam parties in large-capacity clubs in Ibiza
are projected on them. There are also billiard and foosball
tables on which tournaments take place routinely.
The people behind the counter work here fulltime while
they're stationed in the camp. Their duties include stocking
the refrigerator, reordering supplies, opening drink
cans, making change for customers, signing off on ration
cards for alcohol, opening and closing the facility, and,
on a voluntary basis, communicating with the odd soldier
sitting alone at the bar.

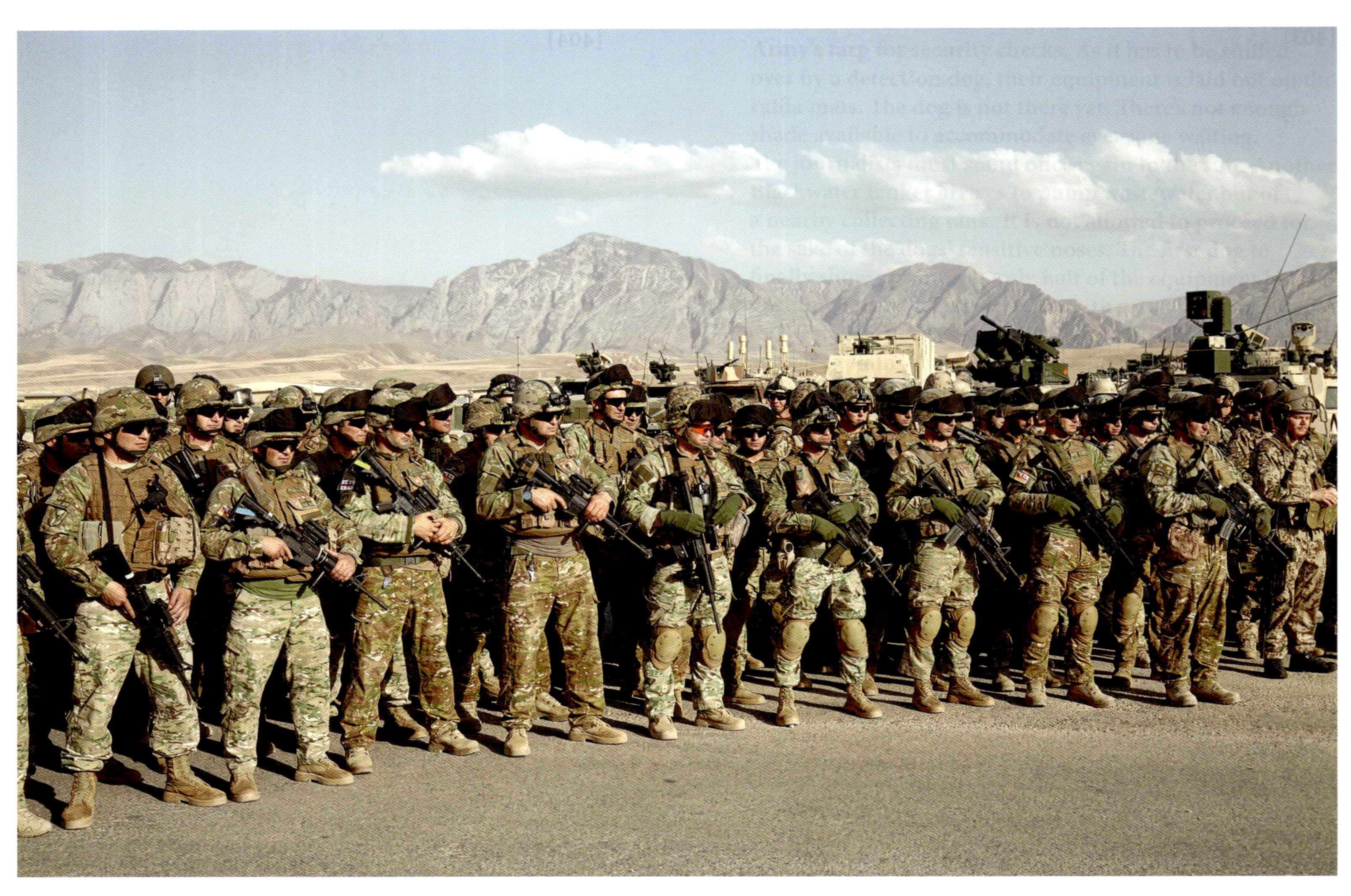

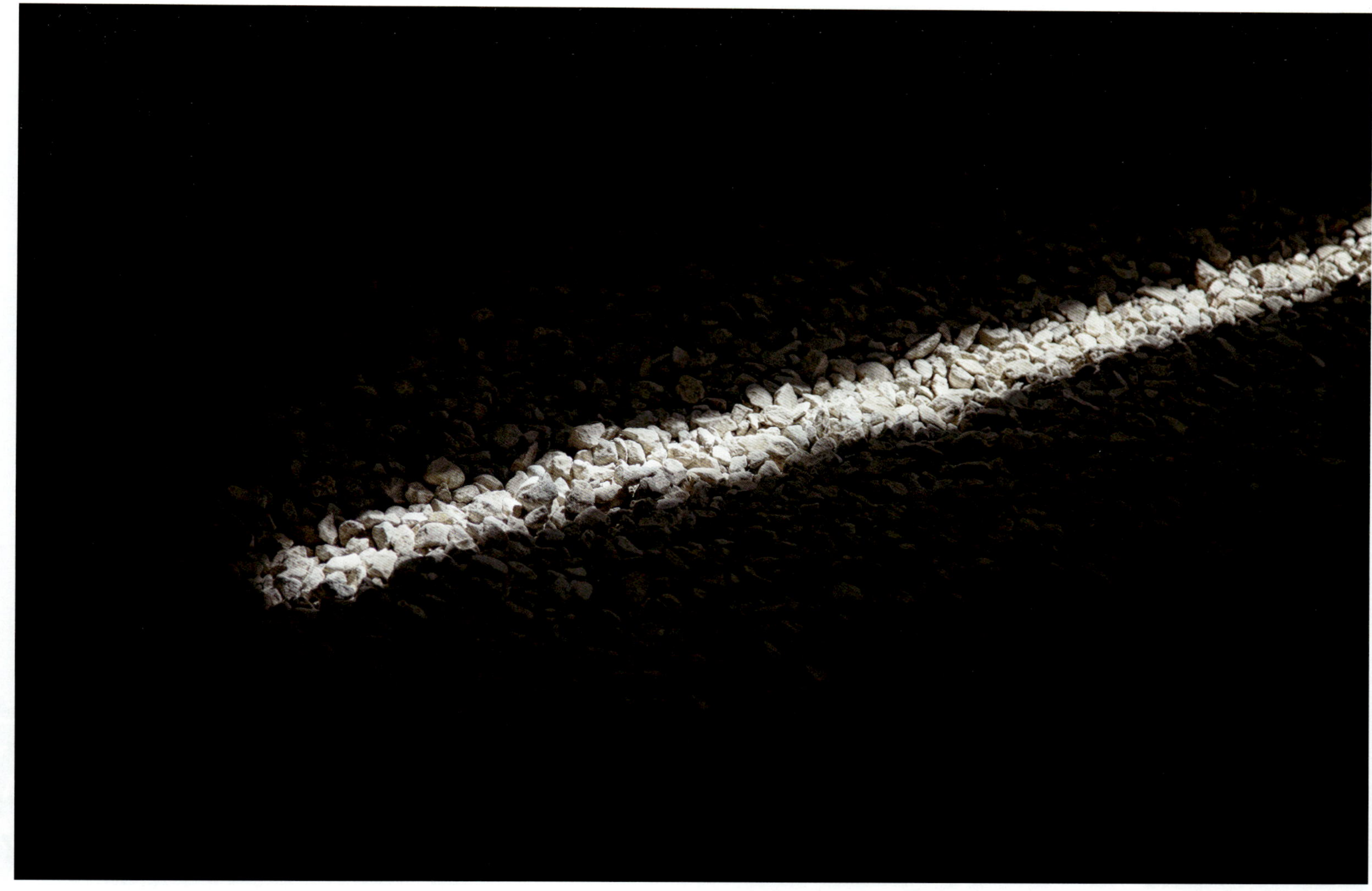

In the *Blaue Lagune*, a small soldier-operated bar attached to the repair shop near the airport, the young mechanic standing behind the counter recounts how, after finishing his vocational training, he began his career in the army due to the lack of opportunities on the free job market. Now he's afraid that once his ten years of mandatory service are over his employment with the military won't be extended. And his work experience as a mechanic has had so exclusively and specifically to do with military equipment that it wouldn't be of any use in a civilian repair shop. In fact, he'd have to go back to school for more training. He's quite upset about the perception that civilian folks back home have of the men and women deployed here. One thing's for sure, says the mechanic as he hands two cans of chilled beer over the counter: he didn't come here to get wasted.

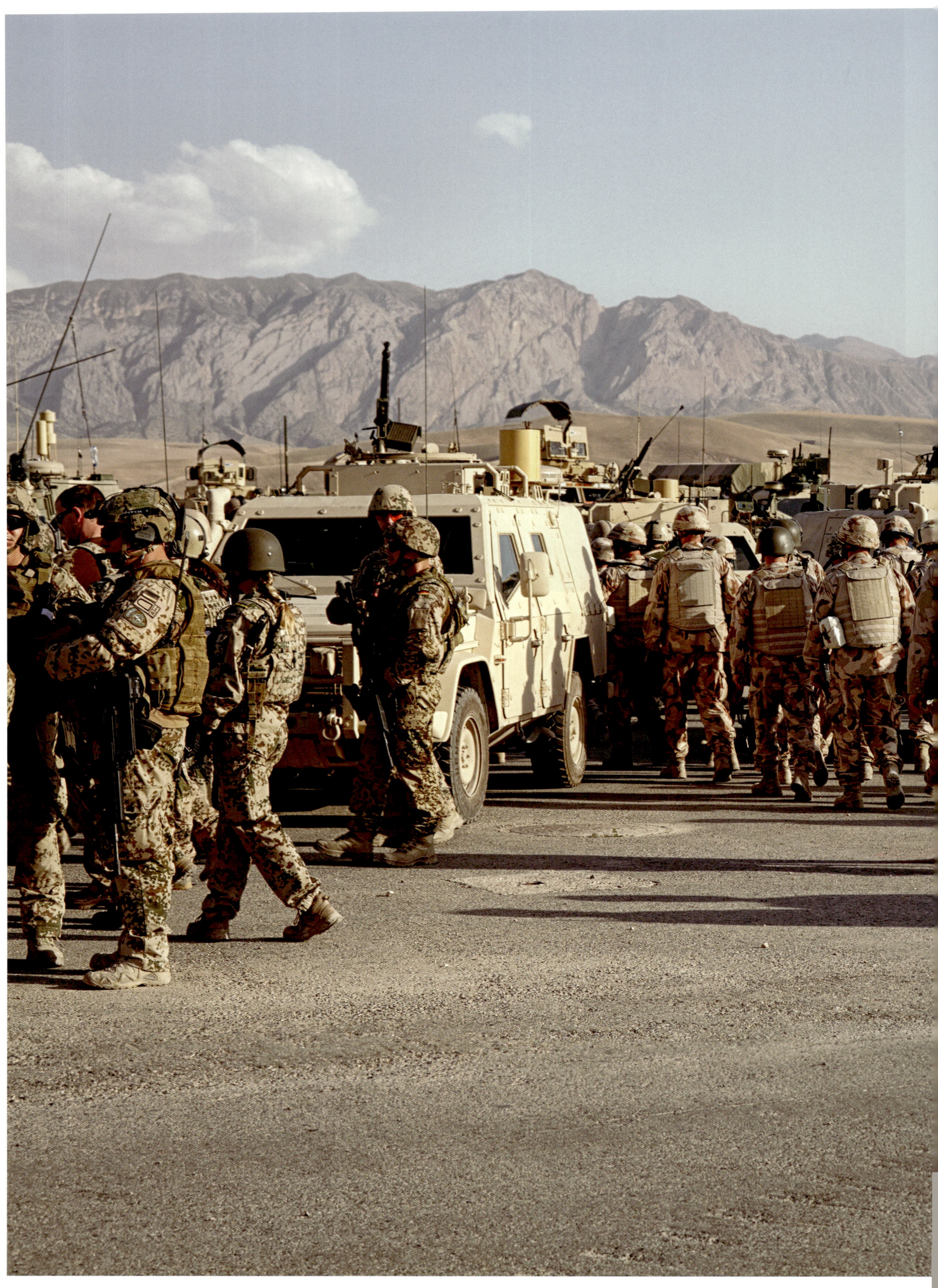

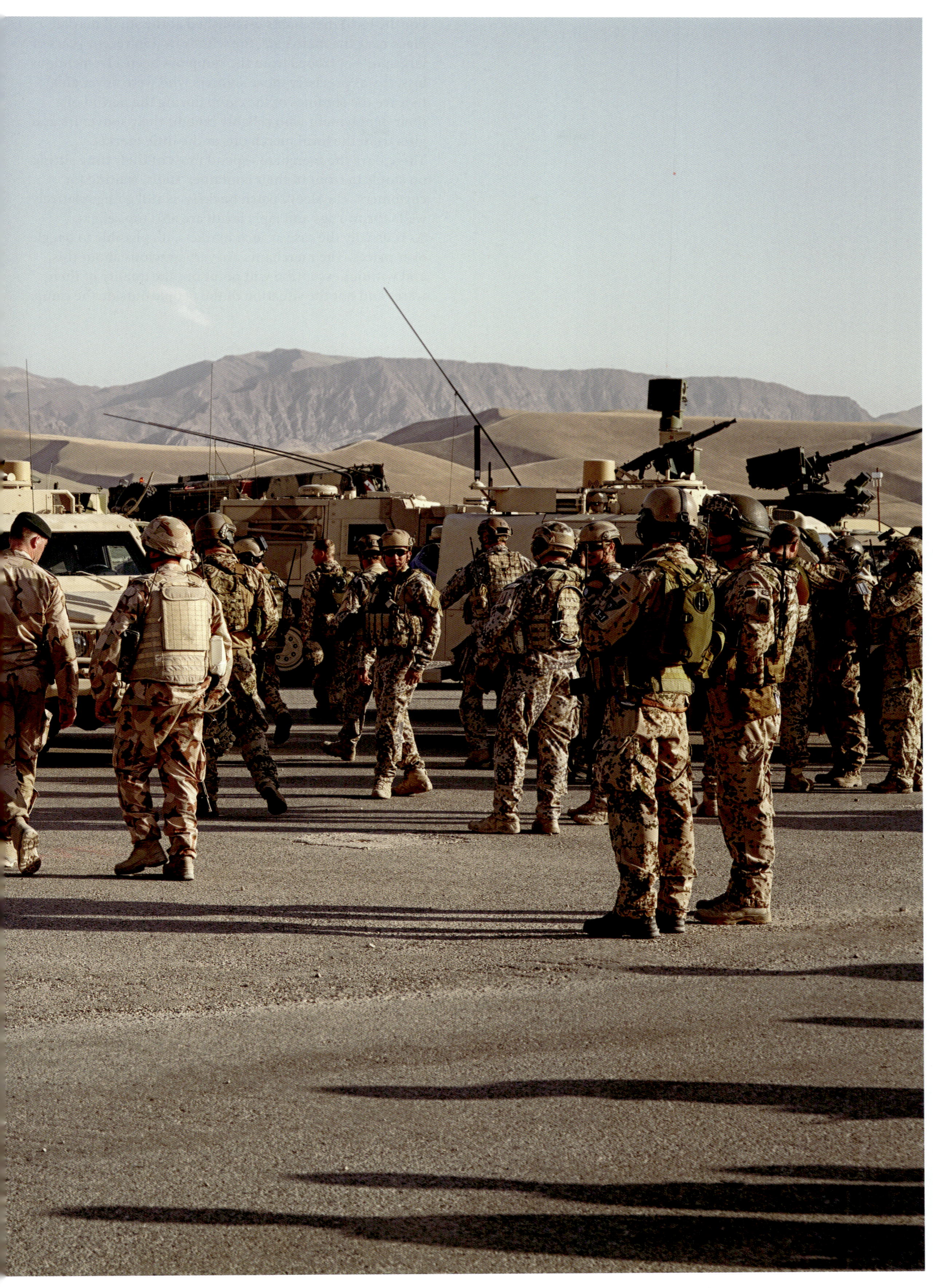

[421]

For the local merchants established at the small market-place near the main gate, the withdrawal in recent years of large units of troops from the camp has been a tremendous loss. It was precisely those soldiers who were never able to leave the confines of the camp during the period of their deployment who reliably bought their souvenirs and gifts from the local merchants at the little market.
These days the merchants spend most of their time sitting on stools in front of their container-stalls, waiting for customers. The sleeve patch business is still going relatively well. Throw rugs and lapis lazuli are also top sellers.
As is usually the case at such markets, it's possible to haggle over prices. The merchants are very gracious about this, and without exception will point out the quality of their wares and not the situation of the people outside the camp.

[423]

[424]

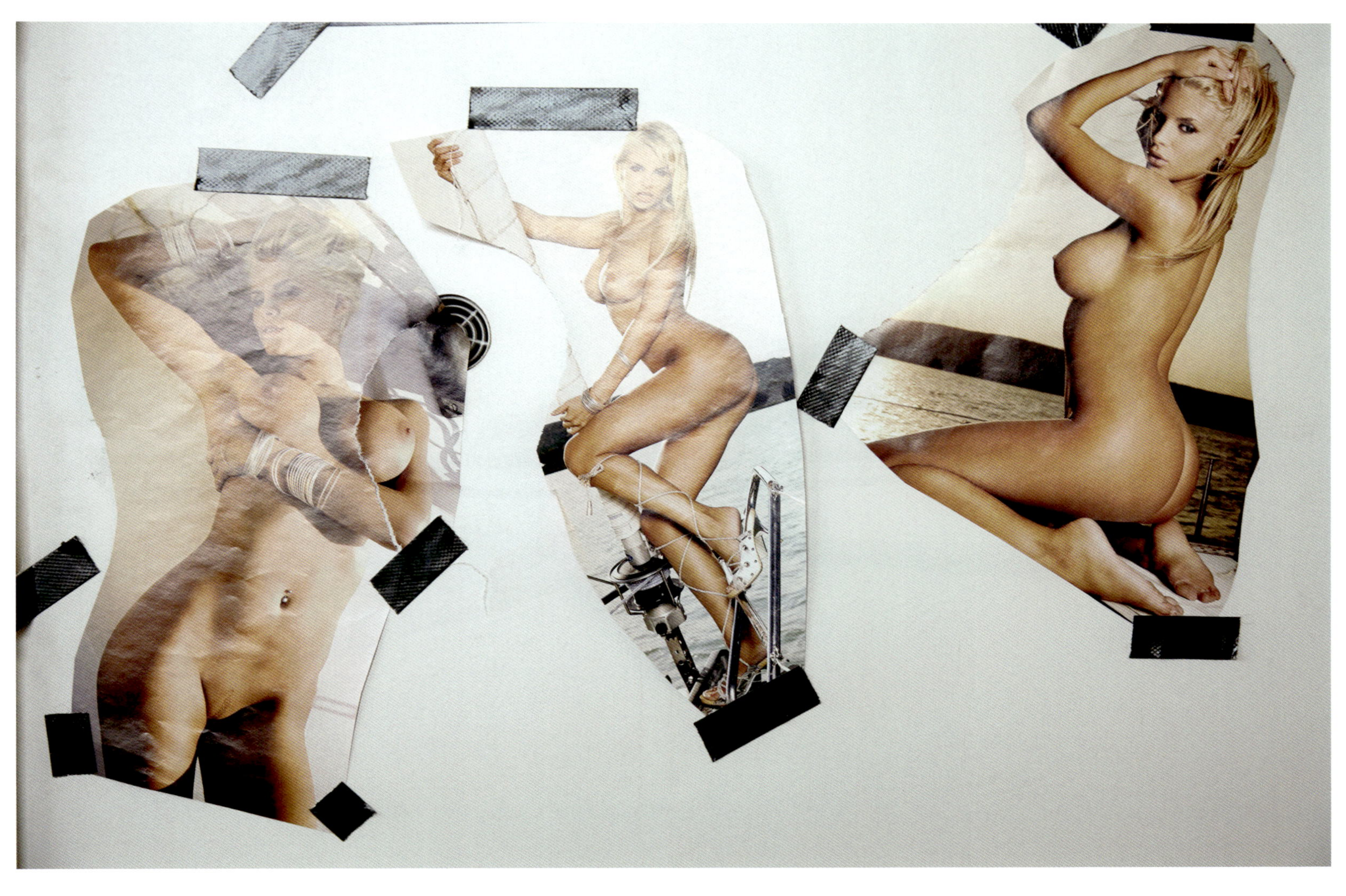

For a number of the soldiers this is already the fifth or sixth time they've been stationed in the camp. Since reporting for duty here is voluntary, some have even taken to calling these people "deployment junkies."

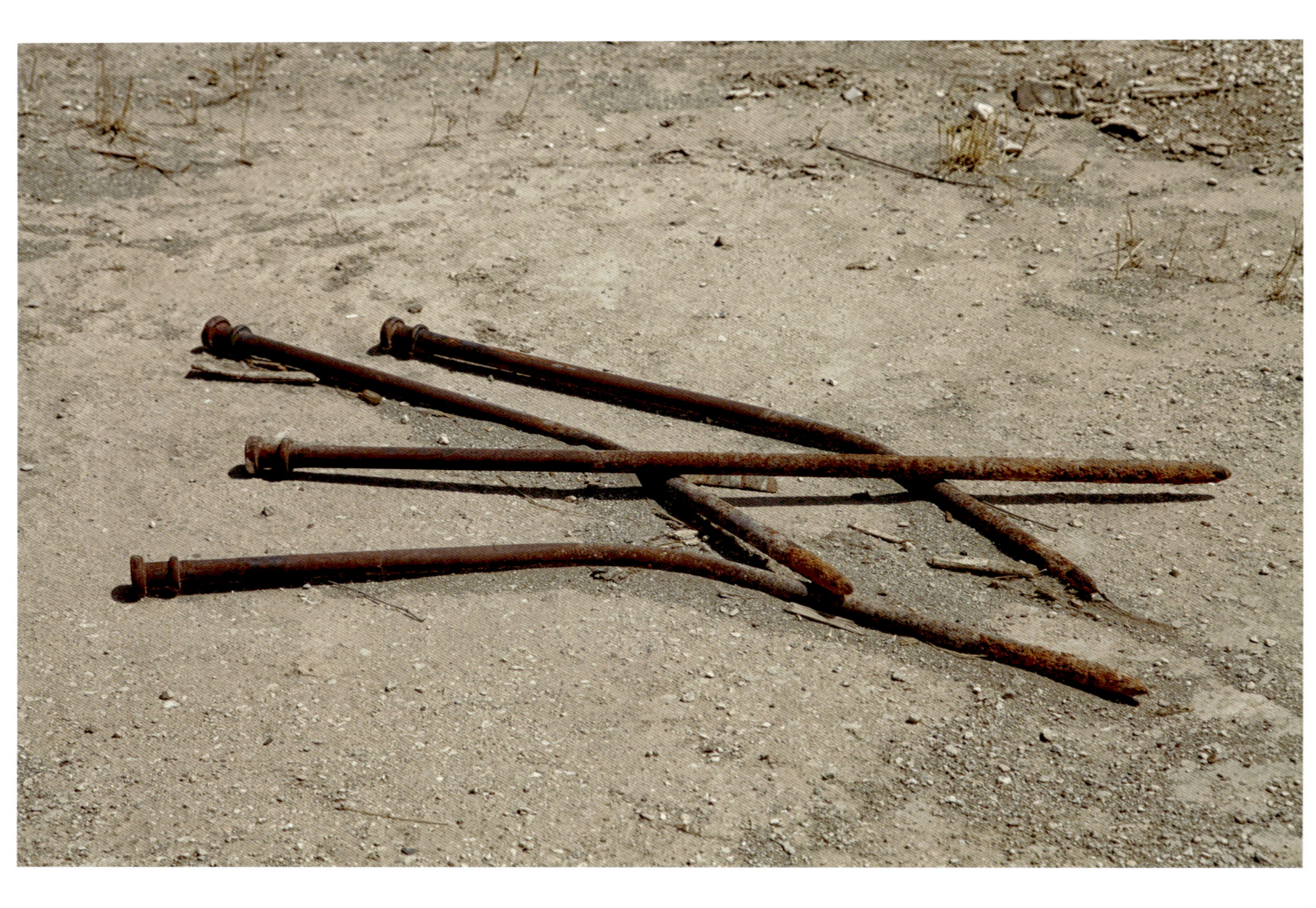

A recurring story: *At some banquet dinner or conference, years after I'd served with him, the General or Colonel So-and-so, having recognized me, makes his way towards me across a room full of people. At the time, he says, there hadn't been the opportunity to do so, but he would like now belatedly to congratulate and commend me once again for the exemplary service. He had really been impressed back then, he says.*

[436]

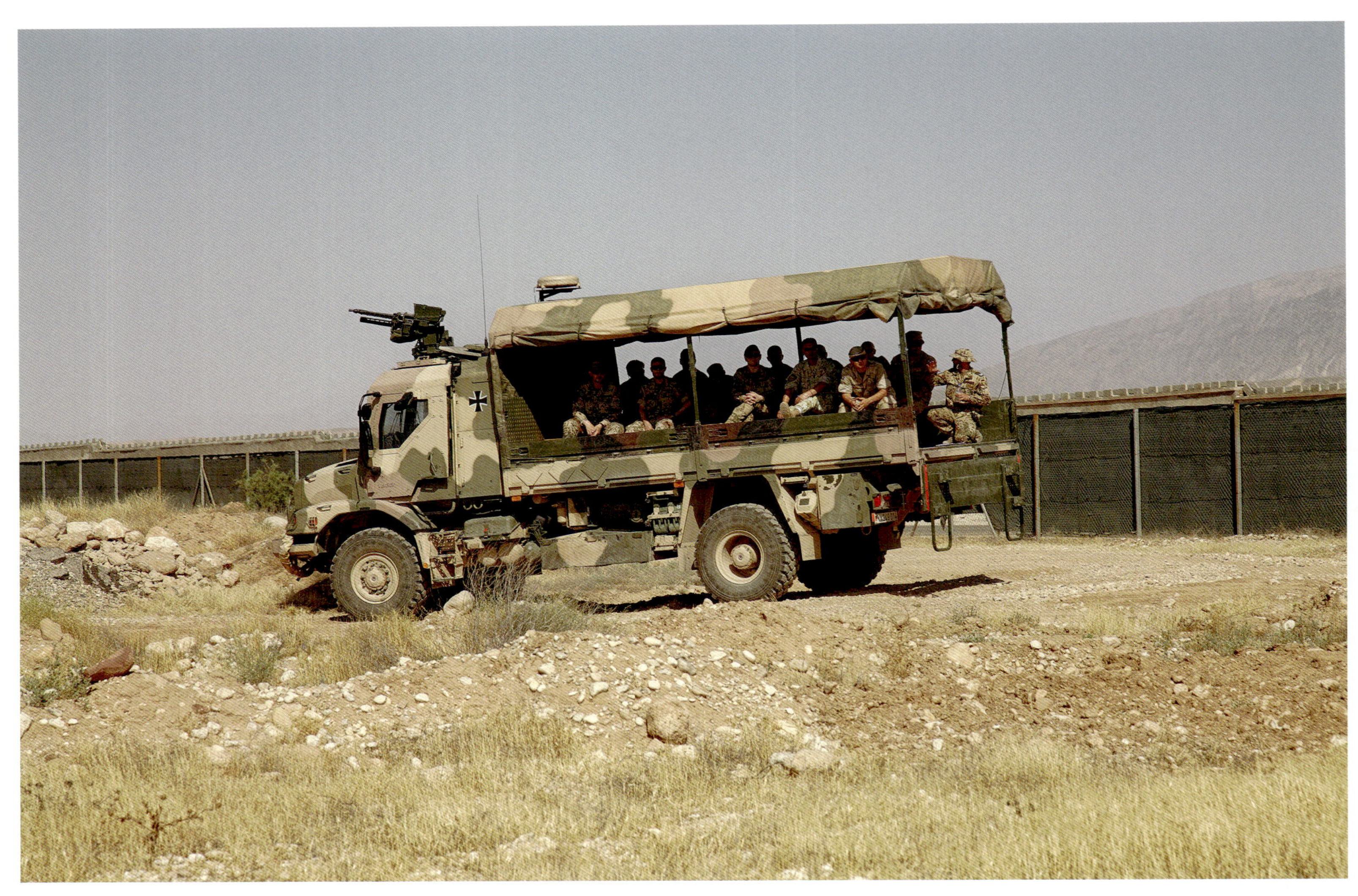

[439]   [440]

On the premises of the camp's sanitation and hygiene department, or *San-Hyg*, the head of camp hygiene routinely leads new arrivals on a tour of the so-called "freak show"—a collection of prepared specimens representing the most problematic of creatures native to the locality: snakes, gerbils, millipedes, wasps (really big wasps), cockroaches, ticks, beetles, camel spiders, worms, scorpions, and of course also, though only identifiable under the microscope, the notorious sand fly. The ticks indigenous to the region have the distinction of being able to detect the scent of human beings and actively go out in search of them. As far as the sand flies are concerned, the head of camp hygiene has held from the very beginning the opinion that the counter-I.E.D. training ground should in fact be cleared completely and resurfaced with gravel in order to prevent their spreading. She shows us a wall chart displaying various cases of cutaneous leishmaniasis with red pustules and weeping craterous lesions on feet and legs. If we'd like, she says, we're welcome to attend the fumigation of gerbil burrows on the counter-I.E.D. training ground scheduled for the following day.

For this purpose, a soldier from the medical platoon climbs early in the morning into an NBC-suit (nuclear, biological, chemical) and fires up a gasoline-powered fogging machine filled with neurotoxin. He continues to apply the poisonous fumes to the entry holes of the gerbils' burrows, until at some point the withered, dried-out steppe grass nearest the hot muzzle of the fogging machine ignites, and a small wildfire breaks out and spreads across the counter-I.E.D. training ground. At first, half-empty fire extinguishers are brought over from the nearby hangar, but these prove insufficient for containing the blaze, so that in the end the camp's fire department has to be summoned after all.

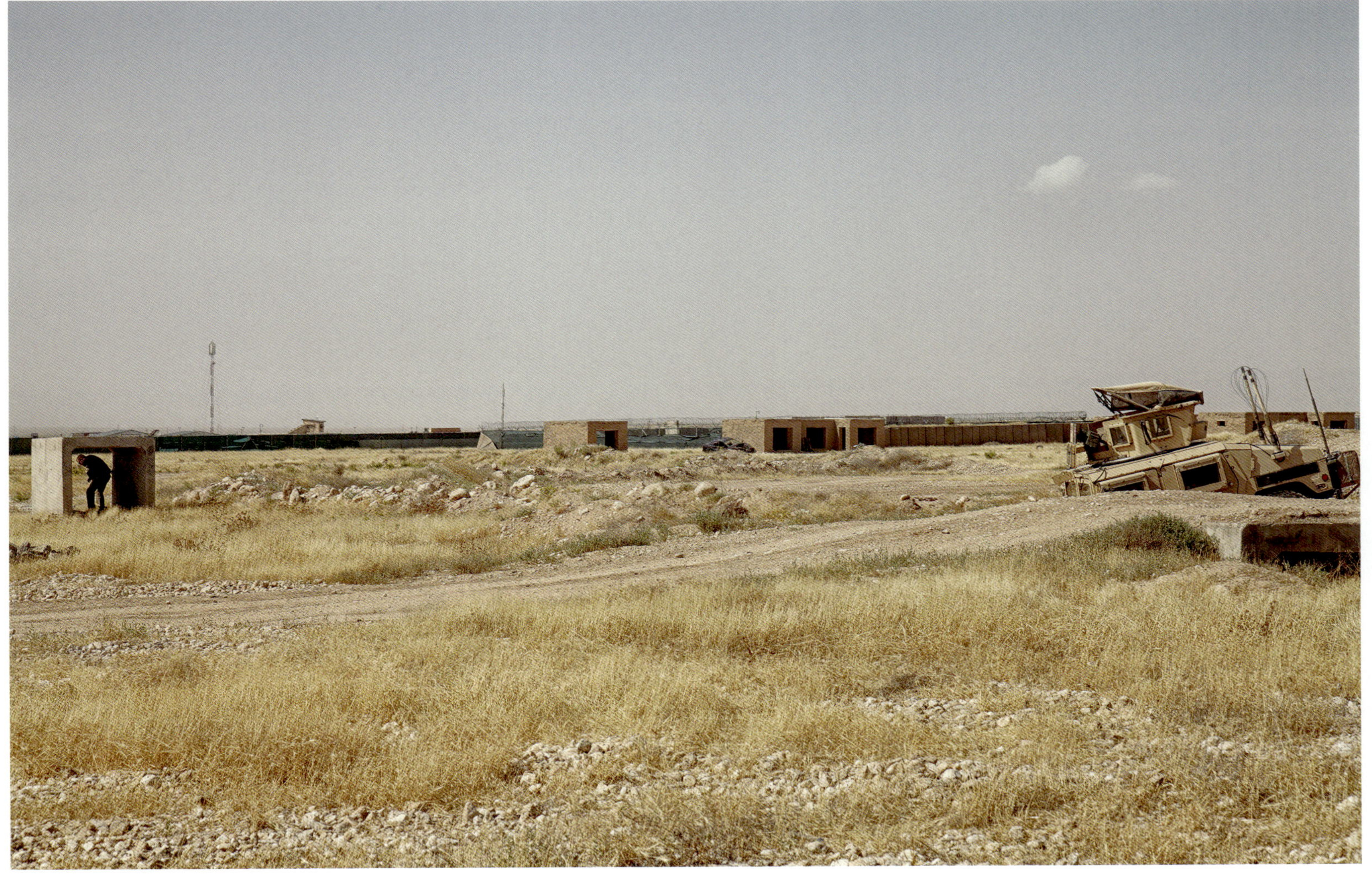

While checking the return addresses on packages submitted for dispatch in the storeroom of the Field Post Office, a disgruntled reservist begins to speak his mind. Both Germany's government and its military, he says, have utterly failed to understand their own situation here in this country. In fact, this very Field Post Office is a really good example of this. For years there's been the problem that all of the independent contractors and companies employed here in the camp do their mailing out of this Field Post Office, and so just like any soldier, only pay the domestic postage for the nation responsible for the post office, in other words, Germany. But this isn't how it was intended to be, he says. The military postal service is there for the soldiers. He once did an audit of one of these companies and in doing so, earned the German military 90,000 euros in additional revenue. Since then, the reservist argues, all the employees of this office have been effectively cost-neutral. Meanwhile, he's now on his ninth deployment. Over the years, he says, "with my work here I've saved the German military at least enough money for an MRAP." MRAP stands for Mine Resisted Ambush Protected, referring to the costly armoring modified to military vehicles.

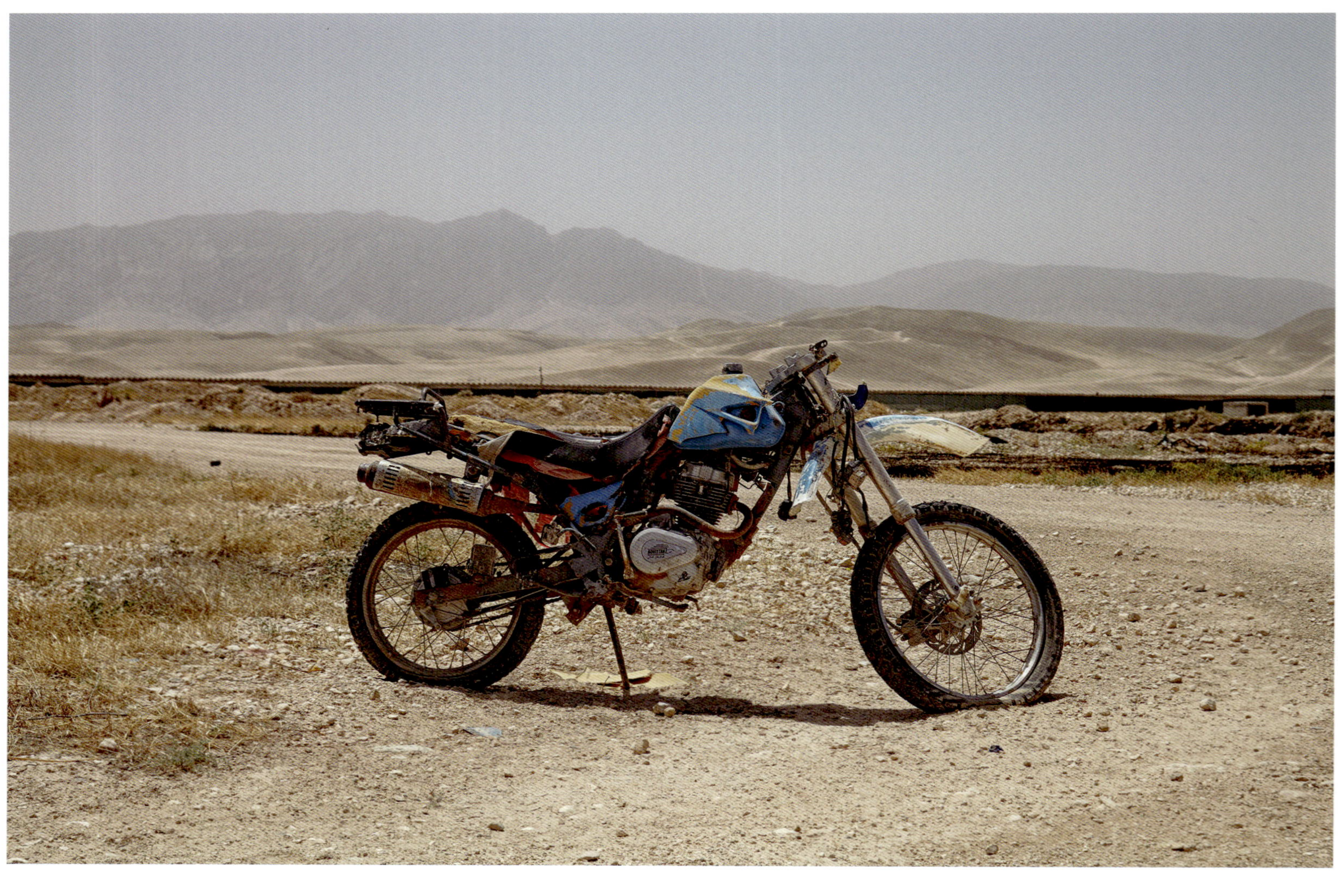

[449]

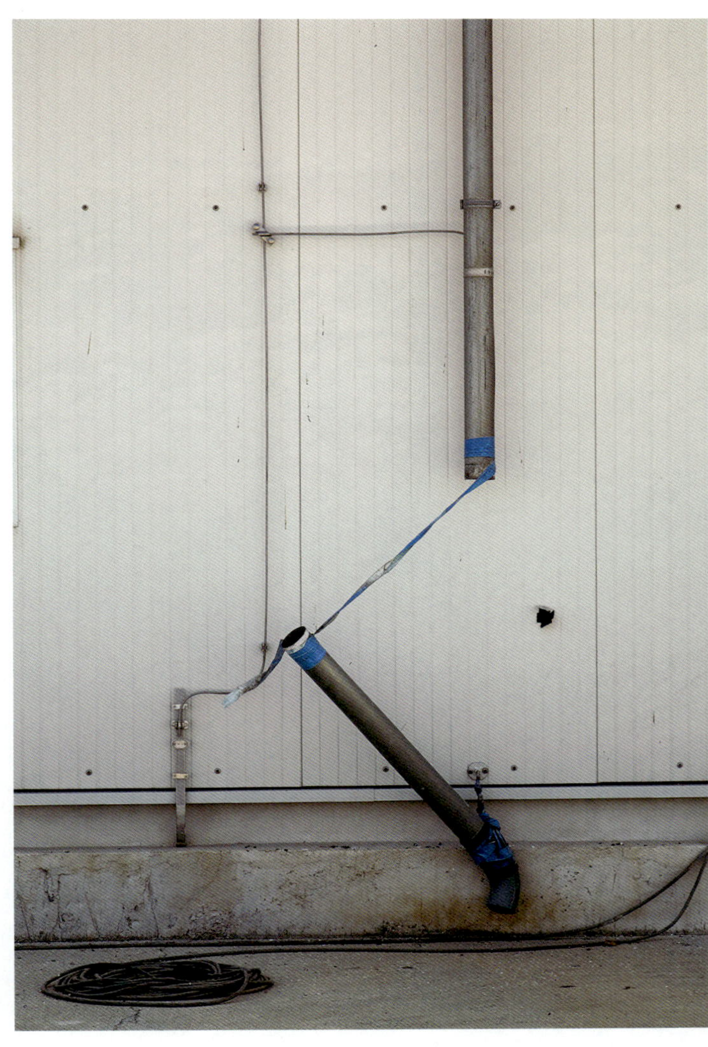

[451]

[452]

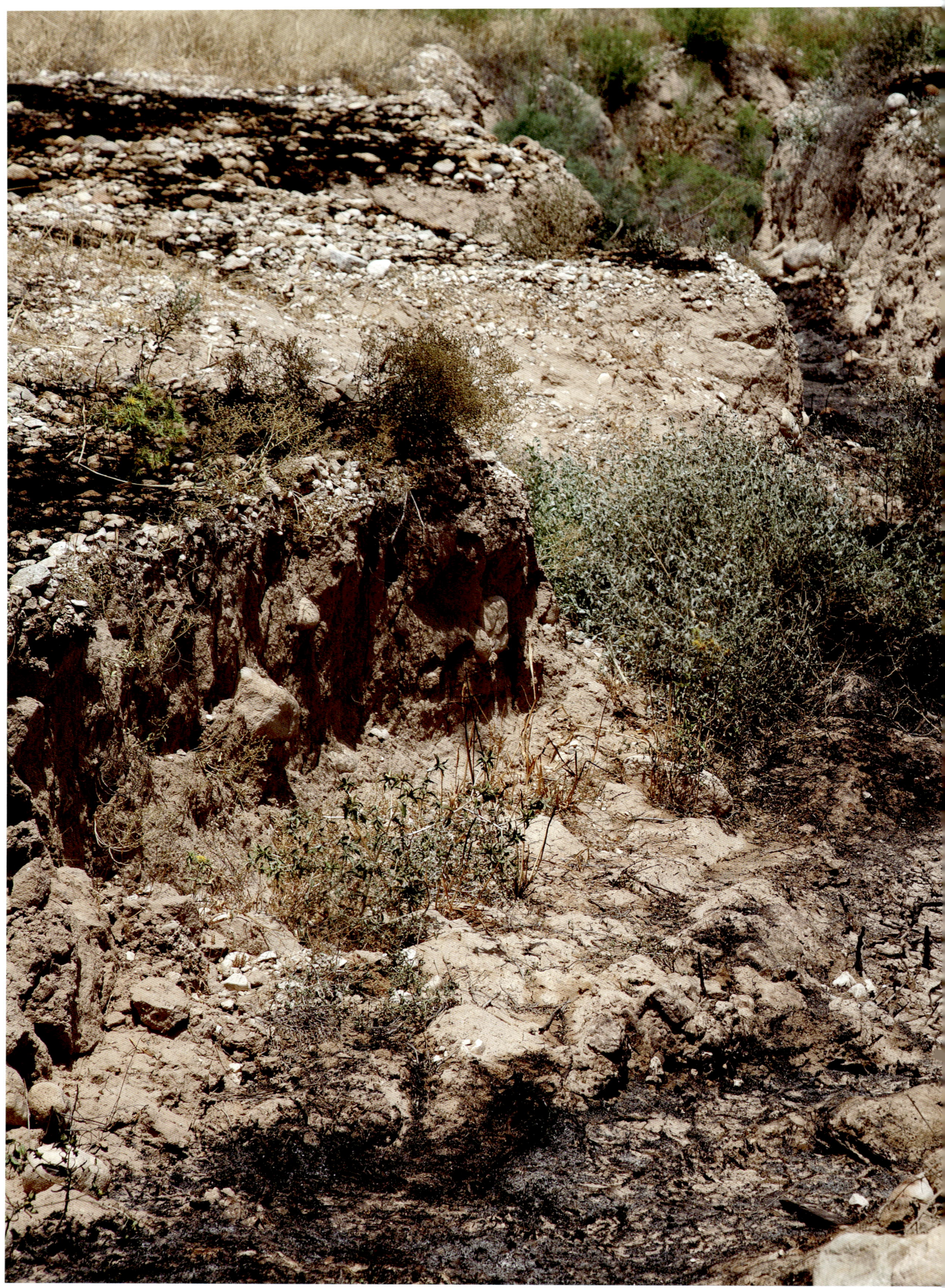

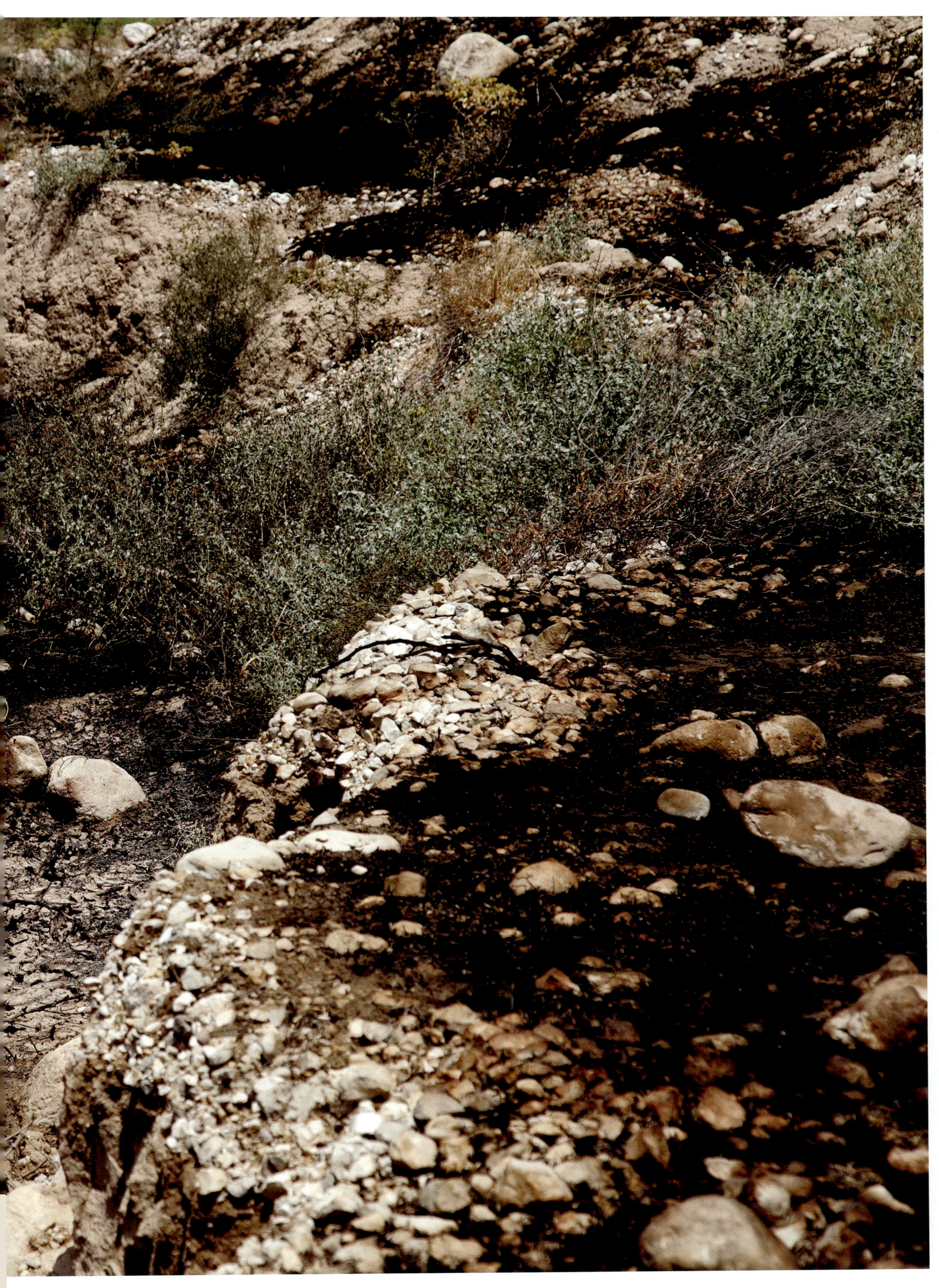

A ceremony is held in the Finnish section of the camp to
honor the memory of a fallen comrade. Guests from
other nations are allowed to participate as well. For the
audience there are rows of chairs sitting directly in the sun.
The ceremony resembles a kind of theatrical production.
Someone comes out from behind a container on the side
and gives the rows of assembled soldiers a command
in Finnish. Then they all rummage around in their pockets,
pull out their cell phones and set them to silent mode.
Additional points on the program include: standing
at attention, shouting in unison, removing of caps, and
putting them back on. During their performance of
this standardized choreography, most of the soldiers find it
hard to suppress a smile.

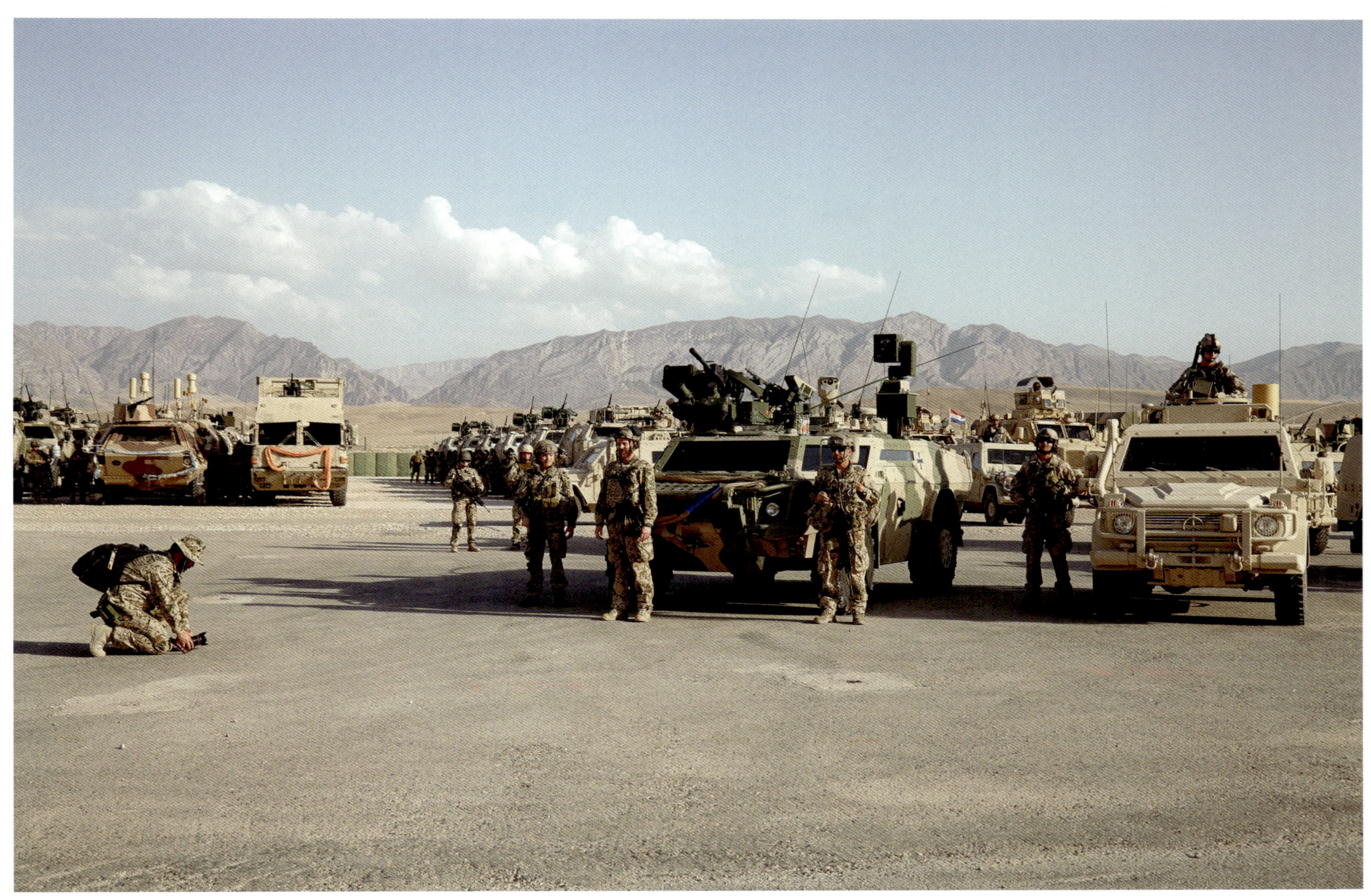

At regular intervals, parties are thrown in the Atrium for the children of the local orphanage. The majority of them have lost their parents in war-related hostilities. On one end of the courtyard, a welcome banner is hung above the stage, gift packages wrapped in silver and gold Mylar emergency blankets piled beneath it—items donated by relatives back home. Some of the soldiers who have signed up voluntarily for this are wearing sombreros and white t-shirts. They let the kids chase them around the courtyard with squirt guns. There's also a mini-soccer field, ring-toss and knock-me-down cans, face painting, and, in the shade on the periphery, a couple of stands where Afghan women sell fabric and scarves.

[468]

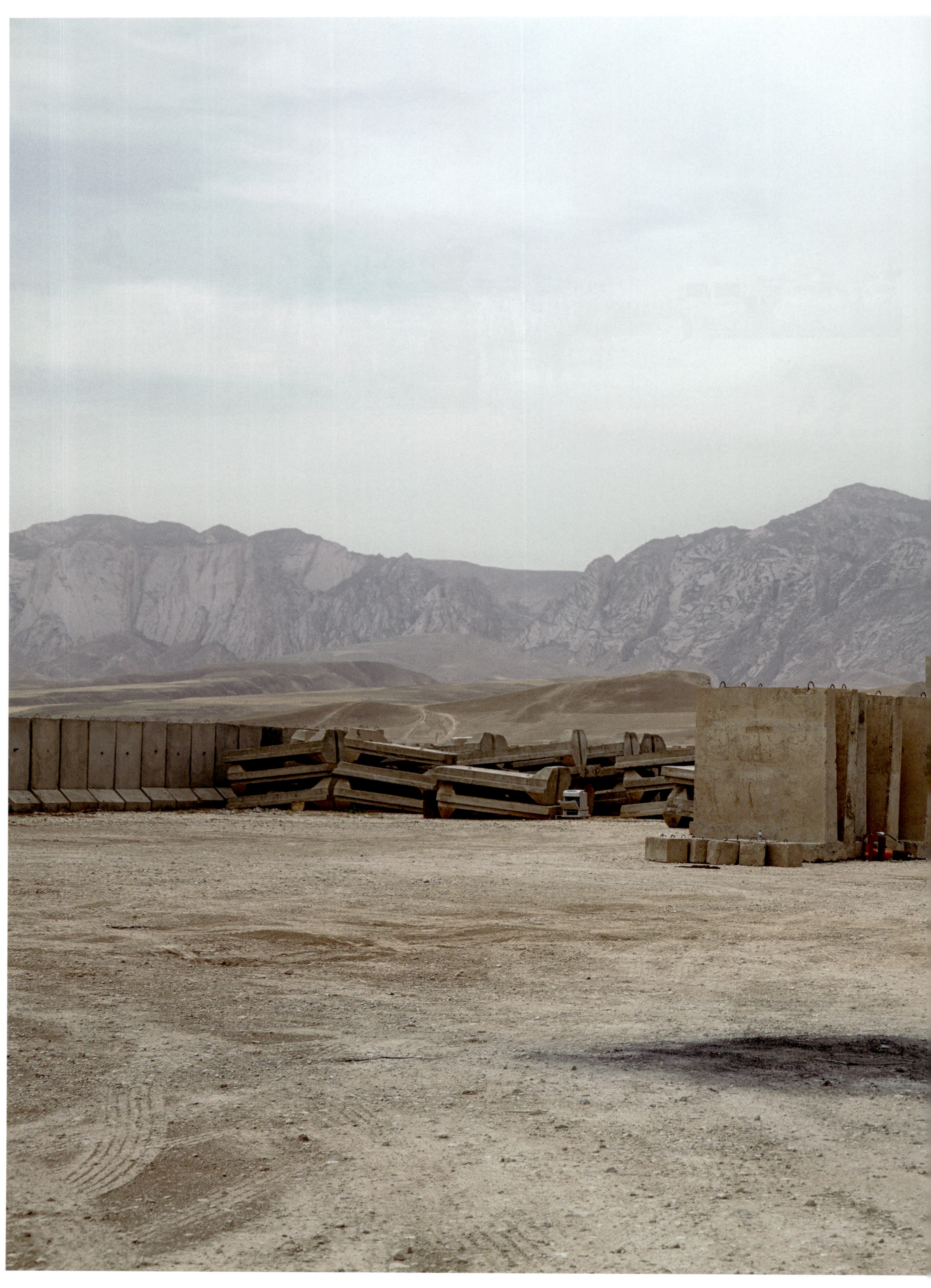

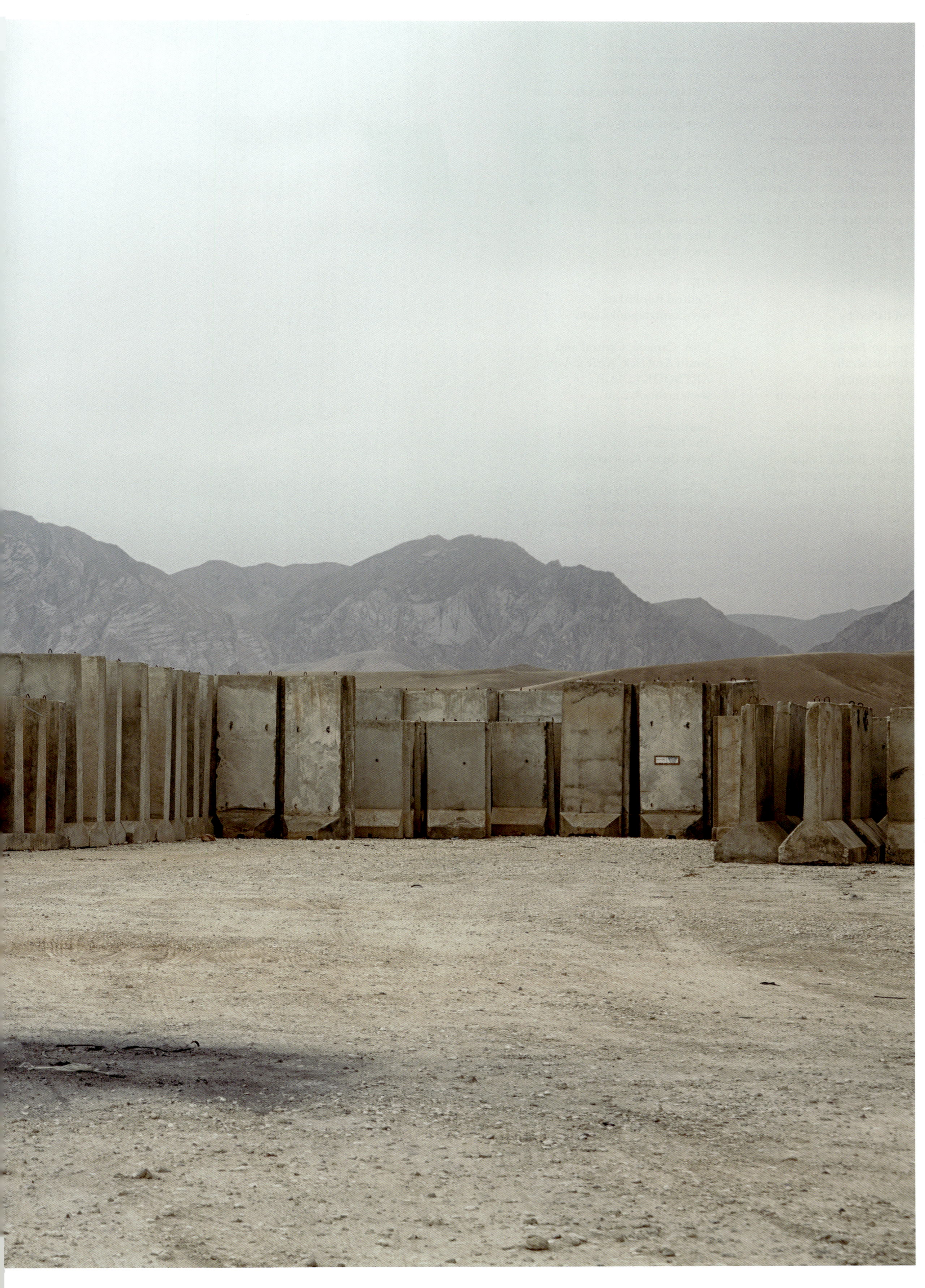

Text: Roman Ehrlich
Photography: Michael Disqué
Concept and design:
Mirja Thomer, Markus Dreßen
(Spector Bureau)
Lithography: hausstætter
herstellung, berlin
Translation: Elke K. Wardlaw
Proofreading: Ames Gerould
Printing and binding:
Ruksaldruck GmbH & Co. KG,
Berlin

Published by

Spector Books
Harkortstraße 10
04107 Leipzig
www.spectorbooks.com

© 2017 Roman Ehrlich,
Michael Disqué;
Spector Books, Leipzig
© 2017 for the reproduced
works by Michael Disqué:
VG-Bild-Kunst Bonn

First edition

Printed in Germany
ISBN 978-3-95905-149-1

Distribution

Germany, Austria
GVA, Gemeinsame
Verlagsauslieferung Göttingen
GmbH & Co. KG
www.gva-verlage.de

Switzerland
AVA Verlagsauslieferung AG
www.ava.ch

France, Belgium
Interart Paris
www.interart.fr

UK
Central Books Ltd
www.centralbooks.com

USA, Canada, Central and
South America, Africa, Asia:
ARTBOOK | D.A.P.
www.artbook.com

South Korea
The Book Society
www.thebooksociety.org

Australia, New Zealand
Perimeter Distribution
www.perimeterdistribution.com

Other countries
Motto Distribution
www.mottodistribution.com